BIBLE PRAYERS

ALSO WRITTEN OR EDITED BY MICHAEL PERRY
(EDITIONS IN ENGLISH)

The Daily Bible, The Scripture Union and Oxford University Press,
various editions from 1980

Living with God, Ark Publishing 1980

With Jubilate Editors, *Psalm Praise*, CPAS/Falcon, various editions from 1973

With Jubilate Editors, *Hymns for Today's Church*, Hodder & Stoughton,
various editions from 1981 to 1987

I, Paul, Creative Publishing, 1986

With Norman Warren, *The Wedding Book*, HarperCollins, 1989

Come Rejoice! HarperCollins, words edition and music edition, 1989, 1990

With David Peacock, *Church Family Worship*, Hodder & Stoughton,
various editions and formats 1986 to 1989

With David Iliff, *Carols for Today*, Hodder & Stoughton, various editions
and formats, 1986 to 1990

With David Peacock, *Carol Praise*, HarperCollins, various editions
and formats, 1987 onwards

With David Peacock, *Let's Praise!*, HarperCollins, various editions
and formats, 1987 onwards

The Dramatised Bible, HarperCollins, various editions from 1989

With David Iliff, *Psalms for Today*, Hodder & Stoughton, 1990

With David Peacock, *Songs from the Psalms*, HarperCollins, 1990

Dramatised Bible Readings for Festivals, HarperCollins, 1991

Prayers for the People, HarperCollins, two formats, 1992

Bible Praying, HarperCollins, 1992

Preparing for Worship, HarperCollins, 1995

The Dramatized Bible, Baker Book House (USA), various editions from 1995

Singing to God, Hope Publishing Company (USA), Stainer & Bell (UK), 1995/6

Bible Prayers for Worship

Michael Perry

Marshall Pickering
An Imprint of HarperCollinsPublishers

To my colleagues in ministry
whose prayers and encouragement
have always followed me – thank you

Marshall Pickering is an Imprint of
HarperCollins*Religious*
Part of HarperCollins*Publishers*
77–85 Fulham Palace Road, London W6 8JB

First published in Great Britain
in 1997 by Marshall Pickering

1   3   5   7   9   10   8   6   4   2

A catalogue record for this book is
available from the British Library

ISBN 0 551 03019 4

Typeset by Harper Phototypesetters Limited
Northampton, England
Printed and bound in Great Britain by
Caledonian International Book Manufacturing Ltd, Glasgow

Contents

Acknowledgements

I would like to acknowledge the early encouragement of Prebendary John Moore, Pat Goodland and Archdeacon Trevor Lloyd, the literary help of Chris Idle, Angela Griffiths and Bishop Colin Buchanan, the Hebrew expertise of Kathleen Bowe in respect of the psalm versions; the patience of my wife Beatrice and of my staff Jane, Gill, Rupert, Andy and Mandy; the generosity of my churches, the ongoing faithfulness of my PA Bunty, the unquestioned skill of my secretary Valerie, the equanimity of my reprographer Dorothy, the persistence of my lexicographer Helen and the major contribution over time of my HarperCollins editors Christine and Kathy. I want to thank the publishers of my liturgical works – not least Rob Warner and Tim Anderson and those at Hodder & Stoughton who took the original risk with *Church Family Worship*, George Shorney of Hope Publishing Company (and colleagues in the USA who promote my hymns and songs and license all my work there), Paul Engle of Baker Book House with Linda Triemstra (and their colleagues in the USA whose marathon efforts have now given *The Dramatised Bible* wider currency), Jeremy Yates-Round of HarperCollins (and his colleagues in the UK) who believed in me enough to commission *Bible Prayers for Worship* as a sequel to *Bible Praying*, *Prayers for the People* and *Preparing for Worship*.

To all these, my humble and warmest appreciation and thanks. Should worship and ministry be further enabled by this book, may they each one derive satisfaction and pleasure from their association with this project.

MICHAEL PERRY, MAYFIELD, 1996

Foreword

I had known Michael Perry for many years, mostly by correspondence and by his writings, before I had the privilege of living near him and working with him in the Rochester diocese from 1989 to 1996, and, for a few months, on the Revision Committee of the General Synod which worked on the famous, if ill-fated, 'Six Eucharistic Prayers' in the first half of 1995. I have had the joy of being present when he has been leading worship using his own biblically-based material, and am one of many who have experienced an exciting new mode of approach to God as a result.

I have also had the deeply moving opportunity this year of taking a glimpse into his own life as he faced his final illness. I think that all who pick up this book and who pray these prayers should do so with an awareness that they have sprung not just from the skill of a Bible scholar or the pastoral gifts of a worship leader, but from the heart of a man who has had to look God's eternity in the face and has responded with faith.

There is nothing here which is not the direct text of scripture. It might be argued that there is nothing here that any Christian could not discover for themselves. But when you begin to work through the book I believe you will be struck by three things:

- the enormous range and variety of biblical text used
- the author's instinct for identifying the 'grain' of a sentence or passage which enables him to make an accurate division between

the call and the response, so enhancing our understanding of the text and our ability to make it our own
- the appropriateness of the passages to the themes they represent – the texts make sense both in their original context and to us in our own daily lives. They allow us to acknowledge our own sin, and so reveal to us God's grace

The material takes you through the logical order of a simple service, and examples of services are provided in the appendix. These demonstrate the use of the materials in a flowing and connected way, and reveal a care in constructing liturgical services which is a model in itself.

So read on, and through these prayers meet with God in the person of Jesus Christ and in the power of the Holy Spirit.

Colin Buchanan
Bishop of Woolwich

Introduction

The principle of responsive or 'responsorial' worship goes back to Hebrew liturgies. It is unlikely, for instance, that Nehemiah (Nehemiah 12.31*f.*) appointed *two* choirs simply to walk around the walls in opposite directions! Ezra 3.11 gives us some idea of the choirs in action, and the response of the people:

> With praise and thanksgiving they sang to the Lord: 'He is good; his love to Israel endures for ever.' And all the people gave a great shout of praise to the Lord, because the foundation of the house of the Lord was laid.

This same response appears in the Psalms 34 times, notably in Psalms 118 and 136:

> Give thanks to the Lord, for he is good:
> his love endures for ever.

It is reported again in 2 Chronicles 5, at Solomon's dedication of the temple:

> When all the work Solomon had done for the temple of the Lord was finished, he brought in the things his father David had dedicated — the silver and gold and all the furnishings — and he placed them in the treasuries of God's temple. The priests then withdrew from the Holy

Place. All the priests who were their had consecrated
themselves, regardless of their divisions.

The trumpeters and singers joined in unison, as with
one voice, to give praise and thanks to the Lord. Accom-
panied by trumpets, cymbals and other instruments, they
raised their voices in praise to the Lord and sang: 'He is
good; his love endures for ever.'

Beyond the suggestiveness of such 'Leader and People' couplets,
the poetic construction of the Psalms encourages – indeed, as
many Bible students would aver – provides for – responsive
('responsorial') use. In their renowned Hebrew 'parallelism' the
Psalms frequently use a further device whereby the first of a pair of
lines makes a statement which is then explained or amplified in the
second, for instance in the opening of the individual (as against in-
tentionally public and liturgical) Psalm 23:

    The Lord is my Shepherd,
    I shall not want.

Or the first poses a question which is answered by the second:

    Who shall ascend to the hill of the Lord?
    He who has clean hands and a pure heart.

There is certainly something very satisfying about worship that
proceeds in this way – statement/exhortation, followed by people's
response; both leader and congregation glorifying God in progres-
sive cadences. The leader thus encourages the involvement of the
congregation, and the congregation affirms the role of the leader.
Such liturgy informs and teaches, yet allows the worshippers step
by step to associate with what is being asserted on their behalf.
Responsive litanies – often, but not by any means always directly

biblical – have a constant and historic role in Christian worship. Their effectiveness is now being rediscovered after a period of experimentation, during which apparently 'unstructured' worship has led to a fresh appetite for 'common prayer'.

Quite apart from the use of Bible type 'responses' after the pattern of the Psalms, biblical worship has usually been the aim of Christian writers of prayers and compilers of liturgies. In recent centuries, free churches, having shaken off the shackles of formal liturgy, nevertheless held on to valuable provisions of the *Book of Common Prayer*, recognizing their fundamental dependence upon Scripture. So well have Bible texts been assimilated in the *BCP* that more than a casual glance at its prayers is needed to reveal how packed they are with biblical quotation and allusion. And their imagery, drawn from the Hebrew life-situations on which the biblical precedents depend, give them a special colour and character. Recent re-appraisal of liturgies (for instance, as Anglicans plan for new texts) have led to a re-evaluation of this Bible basis for prayer. Quite apart from the theological necessity for the Bible to be central to worship, pictures, patterns and resonance matter.

In 1984, a *Jubilate Hymns* team set to work to make further provision for the increasing popularity of all-age worship. The book we planned was called *Church Family Worship*. The compilation was devised in thematic/seasonal chapters, and numbered so that items within them could be used either

1   sequentially as a complete service
2   individually in the context of *The Alternative Service Book 1980*, or
3   as unstructured liturgy.

Although *Church Family Worship* was designed as a composite book (including also hymns and contemporary songs), its prayer material has been widely influential across the denominations. A considerable amount was brought into the Church of England's *Patterns for Worship*. And the majority of prayers, etc. in the now authorized *Service of the Word* and *Affirmations of Faith* stem from *Church Family Worship*.

In 1991 a group of Anglican bishops in Nigeria invited members of the *Jubilate* group to demonstrate to pastors, clergy and lay people across the country musical and liturgical developments from England. As always with such visits, we as tourists learned more than we taught. We offered a variety of approach, but were most certainly affirmed in our belief in the importance of:

· simplicity and picture in worship
· using Bible material as a starting point for hymn, drama, song and liturgy.

Only so could we enthuse church leaders to develop indigenous pastoral liturgies which would meet the real needs of people where they ministered. We returned convinced that what was true in a situation of vibrant church growth was the eventual way forward for most churches that want to grow and to communicate.

Shortly after the publication of *Church Family Worship* I was asked to develop its style of prayer material further. Two books emerged: *Prayers for the People*, and *Bible Praying*. These in turn stimulated further interest, and new requests came from an unexpected source; I was asked to produce Bible prayer material for the worship sessions of the *Spring Harvest* holiday weeks. This current volume combines the biblical prayer material from all these projects, modified and improved and augmented on the basis of use and experience.

The chapter headings explain their contents and follow a sequence which is identifiable interdenominationally. Not every component is present in one worship service – or need be. Within the chapters, prayer material is arranged in Bible order for convenience; and a Bible reference index gives access to the items so that a Bible teaching can be matched and complimented.

The book ends with four sample selections of material (obviously omitting any musical content) for a 'word' service and a communion service.

Traditional Terms

Corresponding to Bible Prayers for Worship *Categories*

Traditional terms listed are those in various denominations most closely allied to the categories used in this book. In each case the traditional words are followed by the *Bible Prayers for Worship* description. Exact equivalents are not possible since concepts themselves change, and because *Bible Prayers for Worship* breaks new ground. But the list is sufficiently accurate to be a useful correlation of traditional, catholic and contemporary terms. It is hoped that the material in the book will be used across the denominations, hence the avoidance of terms which somewhere might offend or prejudice, and the deliberate use of adverbial phrasing for the prayer titles.

1 Vestry Prayer (or Introit, if not musical) – Preparing for worship
2 Seasonal Sentence and Response – Celebrating the season/occasion
3 The Peace/Greeting – Greeting one another
4 Exhortation – Calling God's people to worship
5 Exhortation – Drawing near to God
6 The Commandments – Hearing God's commandments
7 Confession – Confessing our sins
8 Absolution – Declaring God's forgiveness
9 (*No previous appropriate category*) – Receiving God's mercy
10 Exhortation – Proclaiming God's praise

11   Responsorial Psalm – Saying a psalm together
12   Lesson/Reading – Reading from the Bible
13   Sermon – Hearing God's word to us
14   Creed (Affirmation of Faith) – Affirming our faith
15   Intercessions – Praying together
16   The Peace – Sharing Christ's peace
17   Offertory (as applied here to gifts to be dedicated; other
        meanings in parallel) – Offering our gifts
18   (*No previous appropriate category*) – Inviting Jesus in/Coming
        to Communion
19   Acclamations – Acclaiming the Saviour
20   Thanksgiving (also Eucharist here) – Giving thanks to God
21   Administration (recently into 'Ministry') – Ministering
        God's grace
22   Gloria – Giving God the glory
23   Dedicating ourselves
24   Blessing, Benediction – Pronouncing God's blessing
25   Dismissal – Going out from worship

There is no bar on reproducing the material in this book for use
locally, but mention should be made of the source in the terms:

Drawn from *Bible Prayers for Worship*, © 1997 The
Executors of the late Michael Perry, published 1997 by
HarperCollins.

Preparing for worship

Guard your steps when you go to the house of God. Go near to listen rather than to offer the sacrifice of fools, who do not know that they do wrong. Do not be quick with your mouth, do not be hasty in your heart to utter anything before God. God is in heaven and you are on earth, so let your words be few.

ECCLESIASTES 5.1–2

1.1 PREPARING FOR WORSHIP
From Psalm 19, especially Lent
May my words and my thoughts be acceptable to you, O Lord, my refuge and my redeemer! **Amen.**

OR

1.2 PREPARING FOR WORSHIP
From Psalm 19, especially Lent
May the words of my mouth and the meditation of my heart be pleasing in your sight, O Lord, my Rock and my Redeemer.

OR

1.3 PREPARING FOR WORSHIP
From Psalm 19, especially Lent
O Lord, my refuge and my redeemer:
may my words and my thoughts be acceptable to you, Amen.

OR

1.4 PREPARING FOR WORSHIP
From Psalm 19, especially Lent
O Lord, our Rock and our Redeemer:
may the words of our mouth
and the inspiration of our heart
be pleasing in your sight. Amen.

1.5 PREPARING FOR WORSHIP
Psalm 24, especially Advent, Communion, Easter Sunday
Part options: 'E' – enquirer; 'D' – director; or these lines may also be said
by the minister/leader.

The earth is the Lord's, and everything in it:
the world, and all who live here.

He founded it upon the seas:
he established it upon the waters.

ᴱ Who has the right to go up the Lord's hill; who may enter his holy
temple?
Those who have clean hands
and a pure heart,
who do not worship idols
or swear by what is false.

They receive blessing continually from the Lord:
righteousness from the God of their salvation.

Such are the people who seek for God;
who enter the presence of the God of Jacob.

[D] Fling wide the gates, open the ancient doors:
that the king of glory may come in.

[E] Who is the king of glory?
The Lord, strong and mighty, the Lord mighty in battle.

[D] Fling wide the gates, open the ancient doors:
that the king of glory may come in.

[E] Who is he, this king of glory?
The Lord almighty,
he is the king of glory. Amen.

Celebrating the season/occasion

In the presence of the Lord your God, you and your families shall eat and
shall rejoice because the Lord your God has blessed you.

DEUTERONOMY 12.7

2.1 CELEBRATING THE SEASON
Advent, from Ephesians 5
Wake up, sleepers, rise from death:
the light of Christ will shine upon us. Amen.

2.2 CELEBRATING THE SEASON
Advent, from Revelation 1
Look, he is coming with the clouds:
every eye will see him!
Amen.

2.3 CELEBRATING THE SEASON
Christmas, from Luke 2
Today in the town of David is born to you a Saviour;
he is Christ the Lord:
Glory to God in the highest,
peace on the earth!

2.4 CELEBRATING THE SEASON
Christmas, from John 1
The Word became flesh and dwelt among us:
we have seen his glory;
the glory of the only Son of the Father –
full of grace and truth!

2.5 CELEBRATING THE SEASON
New Year, from 2 Corinthians 5
Anyone in Christ is a new creation:
the old has gone,
the new has come. Amen.

2.6 CELEBRATING THE SEASON
Epiphany, from Isaiah 60
Arise, shine, for your light has come:
the glory of the Lord has risen upon us.

2.7 CELEBRATING THE SEASON
Epiphany, from Matthew 1
Jesus is born king of the Jews:
we have come to worship him.

2.8 CELEBRATING THE SEASON
Epiphany, from Luke 2
Christ the light of the world has come:
he is the glory of his people –
hallelujah! Amen.

2.9 CELEBRATING THE SEASON

Passiontide, from John 18 and 19

Behold the man:
Jesus Christ, to be crucified!

Behold the man:
born to be king!

Behold your king:
whose kingdom is not of this world!

2.10 CELEBRATING THE SEASON

Palm Sunday, from John 12

Do not be afraid, Jerusalem; see, your king is coming:
Hosanna!
Blest is he who comes in the name of the Lord!

2.11 CELEBRATING THE SEASON

Palm Sunday, from Matthew 21

Blest is he who comes in the name of the Lord:
Hosanna in the highest, Amen!

2.12 CELEBRATING THE SEASON

Holy Week, from John 1

Behold the Lamb of God:
he takes away the sins of the world.

2.13 CELEBRATING THE SEASON

Holy Week, from Luke 24

Know that Christ had to suffer those things and so enter his glory:
Thank you, Lord. Amen.

2.14 CELEBRATING THE SEASON

Easter, from 1 Corinthians 15

Christ has indeed been raised from the dead, the firstfruits of those
who have fallen asleep:
as in Adam all die,
so in Christ shall all be made alive –
Hallelujah!

2.15 CELEBRATING THE SEASON

Easter, from 1 Corinthians 15

Jesus Christ is risen from the dead:
he is the firstfruits of those who slept.
Hallelujah!

2.16 CELEBRATING THE SEASON

Ascension, from Romans 8

Christ is risen from the dead:
he is seated at the right hand of God,
interceding for us. Amen.

2.17 CELEBRATING THE SEASON

Pentecost, from Romans 5

God has given us his Holy Spirit:
Lord, pour out your love into our hearts. Amen.

2.18 CELEBRATING THE SEASON

Trinity, from Ephesians 3

We are the family of God on earth and in heaven; in him we are rooted and established in love, and filled with the measure of the fullness of God:

**to God be glory in the church
and in Christ Jesus
throughout all generations
for ever and ever. Amen.**

2.19 CELEBRATING THE SEASON

All Saints, from Hebrews 12

You have come to the heavenly Jerusalem, the city of the living God; you have come to thousands upon thousands of angels in joyful assembly; to the church of the firstborn, whose names are written in heaven – to the spirits of the righteous made perfect:

we are receiving a kingdom that cannot be shaken.

Let us be thankful and worship God with reverence and awe.
Amen.

2.20 CELEBRATING THE SEASON

Harvest, from Psalm 67

Let the peoples praise you, O God:
let all the peoples praise you!

The earth has yielded its harvest:
God, our God, has blessed us.

Let all the ends of the earth fear him. **Amen.**

Greeting one another

Greet one another with the kiss of Christian love. May peace be with all of you who belong to Christ.

1 PETER 5.14

3.1 GREETING ONE ANOTHER
From Ruth 2
The Lord be with you:
the Lord bless you!

3.2 GREETING ONE ANOTHER
From Psalm 118
Blest in the name of the Lord are all who come to worship him:
from the house of the Lord we bless you!

3.3 GREETING ONE ANOTHER
From Psalm 134, Evening
All of you who serve the Lord; you who come in the evening of the day and worship in his house, you who lift up your hands in his holy place, and praise the Lord: (may) the Lord, the maker of heaven and earth, bless you! **Amen.**

3.4 GREETING ONE ANOTHER
From Romans 1
Grace and peace to you from God our Father and from the Lord
Jesus Christ. **Amen.**

3.5 GREETING ONE ANOTHER
From Romans 15
Welcome one another as Christ has welcomed you:
to God be the glory. Amen.

3.6 GREETING ONE ANOTHER
From 1 Corinthians 1
To the church of God in ——,* sanctified in Christ Jesus and called
to be holy, to everyone who calls on the name of Jesus: grace and
peace to you from God our Father and Jesus Christ our Lord.
Amen.

3.7 GREETING ONE ANOTHER
From 2 Corinthians 13
The God of love and peace be with you. **Amen.**

3.8 GREETING ONE ANOTHER
From Galatians 1, Passiontide
Grace and peace be with you from God our Father and the Lord
Jesus Christ, who gave himself for our sins according to the will of
our God the Father; to whom be glory for ever and ever. **Amen.**

3.9 GREETING ONE ANOTHER
From Galatians 6
Peace and mercy to the people of God. **Amen.**

---

* Here supply the local name.

3.10 GREETING ONE ANOTHER
From Ephesians 2, Unity
Peace to those who are near, and peace to those who come from away:
through Christ
we can all approach the Father
by one Holy Spirit. Amen.

3.11 GREETING ONE ANOTHER
From Ephesians 5, Advent, Easter
Wake up, sleepers, rise from death:
the light of Christ will shine upon us.

3.12 GREETING ONE ANOTHER
From Ephesians 6
Grace to all who love our Lord Jesus Christ with an undying love.
Amen.

3.13 GREETING ONE ANOTHER
From Philippians 1
From God our Father and the Lord Jesus Christ, grace and peace to you all:
grace and peace to you.

3.14 GREETING ONE ANOTHER
From Philippians 4
Rejoice in the Lord! **Amen.**

3.15 GREETING ONE ANOTHER
From Philippians 4
We greet you all in Christ Jesus:
The grace of the Lord Jesus Christ be with you.

3.16 GREETING ONE ANOTHER
From Philippians 4
The grace of the Lord Jesus Christ be with your spirit. **Amen.**

3.17 GREETING ONE ANOTHER
From 2 Thessalonians 1
Grace and peace to you from God our Father and the Lord Jesus Christ. **Amen.**

3.18 GREETING ONE ANOTHER
From 2 Timothy 1
Grace, mercy and peace from God our Father and Christ Jesus our Lord. **Amen.**

3.19 GREETING ONE ANOTHER
From 2 Timothy 4
The Lord be with your spirit:
grace be with you.

3.20 GREETING ONE ANOTHER
From Titus 1
Grace and peace from God our Father and Christ Jesus our Saviour. **Amen.**

3.21 GREETING ONE ANOTHER
From Philemon 1
Grace to you and peace from God our Father and the Lord Jesus Christ. **Amen.**

3.22 GREETING ONE ANOTHER
From 1 Peter 1
Grace and peace be yours in full measure. **Amen.**

3.23 GREETING ONE ANOTHER
From 1 Peter 5

Greet one another with love's embrace:
peace be to all who belong to Christ.

3.24 GREETING ONE ANOTHER
From 2 Peter 1

Grace and peace be yours abundantly through the knowledge of God and of Jesus our Lord. **Amen.**

3.25 GREETING ONE ANOTHER
From 2 John

Grace, mercy and peace from God the Father and from Jesus Christ, the Father's Son, be with you in truth and love. **Amen.**

3.26 GREETING ONE ANOTHER
From 3 John

Peace to you all: greet your friends by name. **Amen.**
(We greet one another)

3.27 GREETING ONE ANOTHER
From Jude

God the Father has loved you and Jesus Christ has kept you safe:
mercy, peace and love be ours for ever. Amen.

3.28 GREETING ONE ANOTHER
From Revelation 22

The grace of the Lord Jesus be with God's people. **Amen.**

Calling God's people to worship

Worship the Lord with gladness; come before him with joyful songs.

PSALM 100.2

4.1 CALLING GOD'S PEOPLE TO WORSHIP
From Psalm 95, Rogation
Part options: 'M' – first minister/leader; 'N' – second minister/leader.

ᴹ Come, let's joyfully praise our God, acclaiming the Rock of our salvation;
ᴺ come before him with thanksgiving, and greet him with melody:
our God is a great God –
a king above all other gods.

ᴹ The depths of the earth are in his hands:
ᴺ **the mountain peaks belong to him.**

The sea is his – he made it;
his own hands prepared the land.

ᴹ Come, bow down to worship him;
ᴺ kneel before the Lord who made us:
we are his people, the sheep of his flock.

ᴹ If you listen to his voice, you shall know his power today. **Amen.**

4.2 CALLING GOD'S PEOPLE TO WORSHIP
From Psalm 100

Shout for joy to the Lord, all the earth; worship the Lord with gladness; come before him with joyful songs:
the Lord is God –
it is he who made us and we are his;
we are his people, the sheep of his pasture.

Enter God's gates with thanksgiving, and his courts with praise; give thanks to him and praise his holy name;
the Lord is good –
his love endures for ever,
his faithfulness through all generations. Amen.

4.3 CALLING GOD'S PEOPLE TO WORSHIP
From Psalm 100

Rejoice in the Lord, all the earth:
worship the Lord with gladness.

Remember, the Lord is our God:
we are his flock and he made us.

Come to his temple with praise:
enter his gates with thanksgiving.

The love of the Lord will not fail:
God will be faithful for ever. Amen.

4.4 CALLING GOD'S PEOPLE TO WORSHIP
From Song of Songs 2

See, the winter is past, the snows are over and gone; flowers appear
on the earth, the season of singing has come; the trees are beginning to bud, the blossom has spread its fragrance; the cry of the
birds is heard in our land: arise, come and worship. **Amen.**

4.5 CALLING GOD'S PEOPLE TO WORSHIP
From Hebrews 4, Ascension

We have a high priest who has gone into the heavens:
Jesus, the Son of God!

He has been tempted in every way, just as we are:
yet without sin.

Let us approach the throne of grace with confidence:
there we shall receive mercy,
and find grace to help us
in our time of need. Amen.

4.6 CALLING GOD'S PEOPLE TO WORSHIP
From Hebrews 12, All Saints

Come to Mount Zion, to the heavenly Jerusalem, the city of the
living God, to thousands upon thousands of angels in joyful
assembly, to the church of the firstborn whose names are written in
heaven; come to God, the judge of all people, to the spirits of those
who are justified and made perfect, to Jesus the mediator of a new
covenant, to the sprinkled blood of Christ. You are receiving
a kingdom that cannot be shaken, therefore, be thankful and worship God acceptably with reverence and awe:
our God is a consuming fire.

4.7 CALLING GOD'S PEOPLE TO WORSHIP
From James 4, Lent

Come near to God, and he will come near to you; wash your hands
and purify your heart:
**let us humble ourselves before the Lord,
that he may lift us up. Amen.**

4.8 CALLING GOD'S PEOPLE TO WORSHIP
Communion, from Isaiah 55

Come, all who are thirsty; come, delight your soul in the richest of
food. **Amen. Amen.**

Drawing near to God

Let us come near to God with a sincere heart and a sure faith with hearts that have been purified from a guilty conscience and with bodies washed with clean water.

HEBREWS 10.22

5.1 DRAWING NEAR TO GOD
From Deuteronomy 12
Lord, our God,
this is the place where we may worship you;
you have set your name here.
Here in your presence our families shall rejoice,
because you have blessed us;
here we present to you the offering of our lives;
here we pledge our obedience to your laws;
here we pray for our children,
that we and they may do what is right
in your eyes.
Lord, our God,
this is the place where we may worship you. **Amen.**

5.2 DRAWING NEAR TO GOD

From Nehemiah 9

We stand up and praise you, Lord our God, for you are eternal.
Blest be your glorious name,
exalted above all honour and praise.

You alone are the Lord, you made the stars, the earth and all that is
on it, the seas and all that is in them; you give life to everything,
and the hosts of heaven worship you.
We stand up and praise you, Lord our God,
for you are eternal. Amen.

5.3 DRAWING NEAR TO GOD

From Psalm 5

O Lord our God, in the morning we come to you, as the sun rises
we offer our prayer and wait for you to answer. Through your great
love we can come into your house, we can worship before you and
bow to you in reverence; but you are not a God who is pleased with
wrongdoing, you will allow no evil in your presence – you cannot
tolerate the proud, and you destroy those who live by violence or
deceit. So, lead us to do your will; make your way plain for us to
follow, help us to find peace in you alone – to rejoice in you, and
sing for joy. Increase our love for you, and so make us truly happy;
bless us with obedience to you, and let your love shield and protect
us. O Lord our God and king, in the morning we come to you.
Amen.

5.4 DRAWING NEAR TO GOD
From Psalm 78, Communion
Lord, we have faith in you:
we trust your power to save.

You have spread for us a table
in the wilderness:
rain down your blessing upon us;
give us the bread of angels,
satisfy us with your plenty. Amen.

5.5 DRAWING NEAR TO GOD
From Psalm 26, Communion
Lord God,
we are here to worship you –
let your love guide us,
and your faithfulness lead us;
we come to ask for your forgiveness,
to gather round your table,
to bring you our thanksgiving,
and to proclaim your redemption:
receive the praise of your people. **Amen.**

5.6 DRAWING NEAR TO GOD
From Psalm 26, Dedication, Communion
Lord, thank you for this building
where we come for cleansing,
where we gather round your table,
where we sing aloud your praise,
where we proclaim all you have done for us;
Lord, we love the house where you meet us,
the place where your glory dwells:
in the assembly of your people
we stand and praise the Lord! **Amen.**

5.7 DRAWING NEAR TO GOD
From Psalm 27, Communion

Lord, you are our light and our salvation;
you protect us from danger,
you remove our fears from us,
you invite us to worship you.
Our greatest desire is to live in your presence;
here we marvel at your goodness
and ask for your guidance;
here with joyful acclamation we offer
the sacrifice of our love,
our gifts and our lives; here we sing your praise,
here we seek your forgiveness,
here you teach us what you want us to do,
and lead us in safe paths.

We trust you and do not despair:
we know that we will live to see your goodness
in this present life; and we look to you for the life to come.
Lord, you are our light and our salvation. **Amen.**

5.8 DRAWING NEAR TO GOD
From Psalm 63, Communion

O God, you are our God and we long for you; with all our being
we desire you, and our spirits are thirsty for you – we want to
sense you in our worship, we want to feel how mighty and glorious
you are.

Because your love is better than life itself,
we will praise you as long as life lasts;
we will give thanks to you;
we will raise our hands to you in prayer;
we will feast upon you and be satisfied.

In the shadow of your wings we sing for joy; we cling to you, and
you show us your salvation.
O God,
you are our God,
and we long for you. Amen.

5.9 DRAWING NEAR TO GOD
From Psalm 84

Enter through the walls and con.e into the presence of God:
Lord God almighty,
how lovely is your dwelling-place.

Lord, one day in your presence is better than a thousand elsewhere:
Lord God almighty,
happy is everyone who trusts in you. Amen.

5.10 DRAWING NEAR TO GOD

From Psalm 84

Lord almighty, how we love this place where we come to worship you; how we rejoice to be here! With our whole heart we sing to you, the living God.

We are happier still if we always live in your presence, always singing praises to you: happy if our strength comes from you, happy if as we go through life we are refreshed by the springs of your Spirit, being strengthened by you on our way, until we see you face to face.

Lord God almighty, hear our prayers today especially for —————/ *those in authority.* You are our protector and our glorious king, blessing us with kindness and honour, if we do right, you do not refuse us anything that is good for us. Lord almighty, how happy are those who trust in you! **Amen.**

5.11 DRAWING NEAR TO GOD

From Psalm 89

God is the strength of his people, and their glory:
Lord, in your name we rejoice,
in your truth we exult.
Because of your love we can hold our heads up high!

Praise the Lord for ever and ever.
Amen and amen!

5.12 DRAWING NEAR TO GOD
From Psalm 99, Trinity

Lord, you are king, and we tremble before you; you are enthroned
in the presence of your people: let everyone praise your great and
majestic name –
holy, holy, the Lord our God is holy!

Our mighty king, you love all that is good; you bring to us truth
and justice – our Lord God, we praise you and worship before your
throne:
holy, holy, the Lord our God is holy!

Our Lord God, you answer your people when they pray to you; you
speak to us, and give us your laws to obey; you show you are a God
who forgives – our Lord God, we praise you, and come together to
worship you:
holy, holy, the Lord our God is holy! Amen.

5.13 DRAWING NEAR TO GOD
From Psalm 100

Almighty Lord,
all the earth shouts for joy;
and we your people come before you
with joyful songs.
We know that you are God,
you made us, and we are yours,
we are your people
and the sheep of your pasture.
Today we enter your gates with thanksgiving
and come into your presence with praise,
we give thanks to you and praise your name;
for you, Lord, are good,
you are faithful to every generation,
and your love endures for ever and ever. **Amen.**

5.14 DRAWING NEAR TO GOD

From Psalm 113

Lord, we come before you now as your servants, and we worship you:
from sunrise to sunset your name be praised!

You are exalted over all the nations:
your glory fills the skies.

Who is like you, enthroned on high? Yet you stoop down to look at our world; you raise up the poor and lift up the needy.
Lord, we come before you now as your servants,
and we worship you. Amen.

5.15 DRAWING NEAR TO GOD

From Psalm 118

Lord, this is the day you made; we rejoice and are glad in it:
save us, prosper us, bless us
as we come into your house.

You have made your light to shine upon us:
we celebrate, and unite to worship you.

You are our God; we give you thanks, and exalt you:
Lord, you are good, and your love endures for ever.
Bless us as we come into your house. Amen.

5.16 DRAWING NEAR TO GOD

From Psalm 132

Let us enter God's sanctuary:
let us bow down at his feet.

Arise, Lord:
come to your dwelling-place.

Let your ministers be clothed with righteousness:
let your faithful servants shout for joy! Amen.

5.17 DRAWING NEAR TO GOD

From Psalm 143, Morning

Lord God,
as we remember days gone by,
and think about all you have done for us,
our souls thirst for you
and we lift our hands to you in prayer.
Answer us now, Lord,
don't hide yourself from us;
remind us this morning
     of your constant love:
for we put our trust in you,
through Jesus Christ our Lord. **Amen.**

5.18 DRAWING NEAR TO GOD
From Psalm 143, Morning
O Lord God,
make us to hear your voice this morning,
for we trust in you;
show us the way that we should walk in,
for we lift up our souls to you;
teach us to do the thing that pleases you,
for you are our God.
Let your loving Spirit lead us
into the place of righteousness,
for your name's sake. **Amen.**

5.19 DRAWING NEAR TO GOD
From Isaiah 55
Seek the Lord while he may be found; call on him while he is near;
forsake all wicked ways and all evil thoughts. Turn to the Lord, that
he may have mercy upon you, and to our God, who will freely
grant you his pardon. **Amen.**

5.20 DRAWING NEAR TO GOD
From Matthew 17
We are in the presence of Jesus:
Lord, it is good to be here!

Jesus is the beloved Son of God:
we behold his glory.

Let us listen to his voice:
Amen.

5.21 DRAWING NEAR TO GOD
From Luke 24, Evening Communion
Lord Jesus Christ, we are disciples; it is evening, the day is nearly over, and we want you to be with us. As we open the Scriptures, talk with us and warm our hearts. When in your name and at your table we take bread and give thanks, when we break it and receive it: open our eyes, confirm our faith and fill us with joy; that we may believe, and declare to all:
'It is true! The Lord has risen!' Amen.

5.22 DRAWING NEAR TO GOD
From Hebrews 10, Communion
Since we have confidence to enter the Most Holy Place by the blood of Christ by a new and living way opened for us through the curtain, that is his body and since we have a great high priest over the house of God, let us draw near to God with a sincere heart in full assurance of faith, having our hearts sprinkled to cleanse us from a guilty conscience, having our bodies washed with pure water. Amen.

5.23 DRAWING NEAR TO GOD
From Hebrews 12, All Saints
Come to worship the Lord – to Mount Zion, to the heavenly Jerusalem, to the city of the living God, to thousands upon thousands of angels in joyful assembly, to the church of the firstborn, whose names are written in heaven; to God, the judge of all, to the spirits of the righteous, to Jesus the mediator of a new covenant. Do not refuse him who speaks. Come to worship the Lord! Amen.

Hearing God's commandments

The earth is filled with your love, O Lord, teach me your commandments.

PSALM 119.64

6.1 HEARING GOD'S COMMANDMENTS
From Exodus 20/Deuteronomy 5, and New Testament Scriptures
Let us hear the decrees, and the laws of the Lord,
learn them, and be sure to follow them:

'You shall have no other gods but me':
Lord, help us to love you
with all our heart, and our soul,
all our mind and all our strength.

'You shall not make for yourself any idol':
Lord, help us to worship you
in spirit and in truth.

'You shall not dishonour the name of the Lord your God':
Lord, help us to honour you
with reverence and awe.

'Remember the Lord's day and keep it holy':
Lord, help us to celebrate Christ
risen from the dead,
and to set our minds on things above,
not on things on the earth.

'Honour your father and your mother':
Lord, help us to live as your servants,
giving respect to all,
and love to our brothers and sisters
in Christ.

'You shall not murder':
Lord, help us to be reconciled
one with another,
and to overcome evil with good.

'You shall not commit adultery':
Lord, help us to realize
that our body is a temple of the Holy Spirit.

'You shall not steal':
Lord, help us to be honest in all we do,
and to care for those in need.

'You shall not be a false witness':
Lord, help us always to speak the truth.

'You shall not covet anything that belongs to your neighbour':
Lord, help us to remember Jesus said,
'It is more blessed to give than to receive',
and help us to love our neighbours as ourselves;
for his sake. Amen.

6.2 HEARING GOD'S COMMANDMENTS

From Psalm 119

The Lord has given us laws to keep:

O Lord, I want to be strong
to obey your commandments,
and to keep them in mind.
Have mercy upon me,
and help me. Amen.

6.3 HEARING GOD'S COMMANDMENTS

From Matthew 22 and John 13

We pray for strength to keep Jesus' commandments:

'Love the Lord your God with all your heart, with all your mind,
with all your soul, and with all your strength':
Lord, help us to obey.

'Love your neighbour as yourself':
Lord, help us to obey.

'Love one another as I have loved you':
Lord, help us to obey.

In your mercy strengthen us
and move our hearts to do your will. Amen.

6.4 HEARING GOD'S COMMANDMENTS

From Mark 12

Jesus said: Love the Lord your God with all your heart and with all your soul and with all your mind and with all your strength; and love your neighbour as yourself:

Lord,
we have broken your commandments –
forgive us, and help us to obey;
for your name's sake. Amen.

6.5 HEARING GOD'S COMMANDMENTS

From Romans 13

The commandments: do not commit adultery, do not commit murder, do not steal, do not desire what belongs to another – these and all others are summed up in one command: love your neighbour as yourself:

Lord, help us to love our neighbours
and not to do them wrong,
that we may obey your law. Amen.

6.6 HEARING GOD'S COMMANDMENTS

From 1 John 4 and Psalm 139

Love one another, for love is of God, and whoever loves is born of God.

O God, search our hearts;
see if there is any offence in us,
and lead us in the way everlasting. Amen.

6.7 HEARING GOD'S COMMANDMENTS AND CONFESSING OUR SINS

From Exodus 20/Deuteronomy 5, and Psalm 106

Hear the commandments of the Lord:

1 'You shall have no other gods but me':
2 'You shall not make for yourself any idol':
3 'You shall not dishonour the name of the Lord your God':
4 'Remember the Lord's day and keep it holy':
5 'Honour your father and your mother':
6 'You shall not murder':
7 'You shall not commit adultery':
8 'You shall not steal':
9 'You shall not be a false witness':
10 'You shall not covet anything that belongs to your neighbour':

Let us confess our sins to God:
O Lord our God,
we have not obeyed
your commandments,
we have not always done what is right;
in our weakness we have sinned,
we have done wrong
we have acted wickedly;
we have forgotten
your many kindnesses
and we have rebelled against you:
O Lord, forgive us and save us
bring us back and restore us;
that we may give thanks
to your holy name
and glory in your praise. Amen.

Confessing our sins

Then I confessed my sins to you and did not conceal them. I said, 'I will confess my transgressions to the Lord' – and you forgave the guilt of my sin. Therefore let everyone who is godly pray to you while you may be found.

PSALM 32.5–6

7.1 CONFESSING OUR SINS

From 2 Kings 22
Lord, we have not obeyed your word, nor heeded what is written in the Scriptures: we repent with all our heart, and humble ourselves before you:
in your mercy forgive us;
grant us your peace
  and the strength to keep your laws;
through Jesus Christ our Lord. Amen.

7.2 CONFESSING OUR SINS
From Ezra 9
O God,
we are too ashamed and disgraced
  to lift up our faces to you,
because our sins
  are higher than our heads,
and our guilt
  has reached to the heavens.
O Lord you are righteous;
we come before you in our guilt,
not one of us can stand
  in your presence.
Forgive us; in Jesus' name. Amen.

7.3 CONFESSING OUR SINS
From Nehemiah 9
O Lord our God,
the great, mighty, and awesome God,
gracious and merciful:
you keep your covenant of love –
you have acted faithfully,
while we have done wrong.
We did not follow your commandments
or pay attention to your warnings.
Even while we were enjoying
  your great goodness
we did not serve you,
or turn from our evil ways.

Because of our sin
our happiness is taken away –
our enemy rules
    even our souls and bodies,
and we are in great distress.
Forgive us and restore us
for your name's sake. Amen.

7.4 CONFESSING OUR SINS
From Job 40–42
Lord, you are without equal;
everything under heaven is yours:
we are unworthy,
and have to answer to you.
We confess our lack of understanding
and repent of all our sin.
Lord, our ears have heard of you,
and now our eyes have seen you;
in Jesus our Redeemer. Amen.

7.5 CONFESSING OUR SINS
From Psalm 41
O Lord, have mercy on us,
for we have sinned against you;
we have suffered the malice of our enemies
and the opposition of our friends.

Lord, we pray,
uphold us in innocence
and keep us in your presence for ever;
through Jesus Christ our Lord. Amen.

7.6 CONFESSING OUR SINS
From Psalm 41, social responsibility
Lord, have mercy on us,
for we have sinned against you;
we have failed to care for the weak,
and have fallen into sin.
O Lord, have mercy on us
and raise us up;
uphold us in the truth
and keep us in your presence for ever;
for Jesus' sake. Amen.

7.7 CONFESSING OUR SINS
From Psalm 51
Lord God, have mercy on us.
According to your steadfast love;
and in your abundant mercy,
blot out our transgressions;
cleanse us from our sin,
create in us a clean heart and life,
and continually renew a right spirit within us.
Amen.

7.8 CONFESSING OUR SINS
From Psalm 51
O God, in your goodness have mercy on us, wash us clean from
our guilt:
purify us from our sin.

We know our faults well:
our sins hang heavy upon us.

Against you only have we sinned:
we have done evil in your sight.

So you are right to judge us:
you are justified in condemning us.

Remove our sin and we will be clean:
wash us,
and we will be whiter than snow.

Hide your face from our sins:
wipe out all our guilt
through Jesus Christ our Lord. Amen.

7.9 CONFESSING OUR SINS

From Psalm 51
The sacrifices of God are a broken spirit; a broken and contrite heart, O God, you will not despise. O God, in your unfailing love:
have mercy on us.

We know our transgressions, and our sin is ever before us; against you only have we sinned and done what is evil in your sight. O God, in your unfailing love:
have mercy on us.

According to your great compassion blot out our transgressions, wash away all our iniquity and cleanse us from our sin. O God, in your unfailing love:
have mercy on us.

Cleanse us, and we shall be clean;
wash us,
and we shall be whiter than snow;
through Jesus Christ our Lord. Amen.

7.10 CONFESSING OUR SINS

From Psalm 101

Lord God, our hearts are guilty,
we have been dishonest,
we have looked on evil,
we have clung to our selfish ways.
We have talked about others
    behind their backs
with haughty eyes and a proud heart.
Lord, forgive us and help us;
renew us in righteousness
    every morning:
make our lives faithful
and our talk blameless
that we may live in your presence
    for ever;
through Jesus Christ our Lord. Amen.

7.11 CONFESSING OUR SINS

From Psalm 109

O Lord, we need you:
our hearts are wounded,
our days fade like evening shadows,
we are weak and despise ourselves;
for we have sinned against you.
Forgive us, O Lord,
and in your constant love save us;
through Jesus our redeemer. Amen.

7.12 CONFESSING OUR SINS
From Psalm 119 and Mark 12

Hear the words of Jesus: Love the Lord your God with all your heart and with all your soul and with all your mind and with all your strength; and love your neighbour as yourself:

Let us confess our sins:

Lord, we are to blame,
for we have not followed your law,
we have not kept your commandments,
we have not sought for you
    with all our heart,
we have not walked in your ways,
nor have we fully obeyed you;
Lord, we long to be faithful
    and obedient:
do not put us to shame.
Give us upright hearts,
teach us obedience
and do not forsake us for ever. Amen.

7.13 CONFESSING OUR SINS

From Psalm 130

Out of the depths, O Lord, we cry to you. O Lord, hear our voice:
listen to our cry for mercy.

If you kept a record of our sins, who could stand before you?
O Lord, hear our voice:
listen to our cry for mercy.

But you offer forgiveness, and therefore we fear you, O Lord, hear
our voice:
listen to our cry for mercy.

We wait for you, O Lord, and we put our hope in your promise.
O Lord, hear our voice:
listen to our cry for mercy.

We long for you, O Lord, more than the sleepless long for the
morning. O Lord, hear our voice:
listen to our cry for mercy.

O God, we put our trust in you,
because with you there is unfailing love
and full redemption from all our sins,
through our Saviour Jesus Christ. Amen.

7.14 CONFESSING OUR SINS

From Psalm 130

O Lord, out of the depths we pray to you:
O Lord, hear our voice,
open your ears to our cry for mercy.

Lord, if you kept a list of our sins, none of us could stand before you:
But with you there is forgiveness;
therefore, we worship you. Amen.

Serve the Lord, wait for him:
his promise is our hope;
in Jesus Christ. Amen.

7.15 CONFESSING OUR SINS

From Psalm 130

O Lord, we cry to you
     from the depths of our being:
let your ears be open
     as we plead for mercy.
If you kept a record of our sins
none of us could stand before you;
but you alone can forgive us,
therefore we come to you in awe.
Lord, we wait for you
and in your promise we put our hope;
through our saviour Jesus Christ. Amen.

7.16 CONFESSING OUR SINS
From Psalm 142

Lord, we have sinned:
we lift up our voice to you
and cry for mercy.
There is no one else
      to whom we can go:
save us from our sins
and from temptations
      that are too strong for us.
Set us free,
that we may praise your name;
through Jesus Christ our Lord. Amen.

7.17 CONFESSING OUR SINS
From Psalm 143

O God, we have failed you; darkness overtakes us – our spirits tremble and our hearts are dismayed; your face is hidden from us and we wait for your word of love:

Lord, hear our prayer,
listen to our cry for mercy;
in your faithfulness and righteousness
come to our relief.
Do not bring us to judgement –
for no one living
      is righteous before you;
show us the way we should go,
teach us to do your will
and let your Spirit lead us;
through Jesus Christ our Lord. Amen.

7.18 CONFESSING OUR SINS
From Isaiah 6

O Lord our God,
enthroned on high,
filling the whole earth with your glory:
holy, holy, holy is your name.
Our eyes have seen the King,
the Lord almighty;
but our lips are unclean.
We cry to you in our sinfulness
to take our guilt away,
through Jesus Christ our Lord. Amen.

7.19 CONFESSING OUR SINS
From Isaiah 43

O Lord our God, we confess
that we have not called upon you,
we have not been generous
        in our giving,
nor have we honoured you;
but we have wearied you
        with our wrongdoing
and burdened you with our offences:
blot out our transgressions
and remember our sin no more,
for your name's sake. Amen.

7.20 CONFESSING OUR SINS
From Isaiah 57

O God,
you are eternal, and your name is holy;
you live in a high and holy place –
yet also with the humble and penitent:
revive our spirits and renew our hearts.
We confess our greed
    and our wilful ways:
you have punished us,
you have hidden your face from us.
O God, forgive us,
through Jesus Christ our Lord. Amen.

7.21 CONFESSING OUR SINS
From Isaiah 63

God, our Father,
we have strayed from your ways;
we have been stubborn
and have turned away from you.
You are
    the one who has always rescued us:
look upon us from heaven
    where you live in holiness and glory;
show your love for us,
show your power,
show your mercy.
For our sake, who love you –
for our sake, who are your people,
return to us and forgive;
through Jesus Christ our Lord. Amen.

7.22 CONFESSING OUR SINS

From Isaiah 64

Sovereign Lord,
we have continually sinned against you;
and have become unclean –
all our righteous acts
    are like filthy rags.
We shrivel up like leaves,
and our sins sweep us away.
Yet, O Lord, you are our Father:
do not remember our sins for ever.
We are your people:
look upon us, we pray,
and forgive us;
through Jesus our redeemer. Amen.

7.23 CONFESSING OUR SINS

From Jeremiah 14

O Lord,
we acknowledge our own wickedness
and the guilt of our society;
we have sinned against you.
For the sake of your name
do not despise us;
remember your covenant with us
    in Jesus our redeemer,
and forgive us our sin;
for his name's sake. Amen.

7.24 CONFESSING OUR SINS

From Lamentations 5

Remember, O Lord,
your people in their sorrow;
look, and see our disgrace:
joy is gone from our hearts;
our dancing has turned to mourning,
we are no longer proud –
the crown has fallen from our head
for we have sinned.
You, O Lord, reign for ever,
your throne endures to every generation:
do not forget us now,
do not forsake us for long:
forgive us, restore us and renew us;
through our redeemer, Jesus Christ. Amen.

7.25 CONFESSING OUR SINS

From Daniel 9

O Lord our God, you brought your people out of slavery with a mighty hand, and made for yourself a name which endures to this day:

We have sinned, we have done wrong. O Lord, hear:
O Lord, forgive!

In keeping with all your righteous acts, turn away your anger from your people. O Lord, hear:
O Lord, forgive!

Our sins have made us despised by those around us. O Lord, hear:
O Lord, forgive!

We do not come before you because we are righteous; but because
of your great mercy: O Lord; hear:
O Lord: forgive!

O Lord our God, do not delay
but send your Holy Spirit
to revive your church,
because your people
bear the name of Christ. Amen.

7.26 CONFESSING OUR SINS
From Hosea 14, Lent
O Lord our God,
our sins have been our downfall,
but now we turn to you
and confess them:
forgive us our sins
and receive our prayer
that we may praise you once again;
through Jesus Christ our Lord. Amen.

7.27 CONFESSING OUR SINS
From Amos 2
Lord God almighty,
we have rejected your law,
and have not obeyed
    your commandments;
we have ignored the needs of the poor,
and denied justice to the oppressed.
Lord, we have sinned
and dishonoured your holy name:
have mercy on us;
for Jesus' sake. Amen.

7.28 CONFESSING OUR SINS

From Jonah 2

O Lord our God,
in distress we call to you;
from the depths we cry for help –
the storm swirls around us,
our troubles threaten to engulf us.
We feel we have been banished from your sight,
but we look again
towards your loving peace.
We have clung to worthless things
and forfeited the grace
    that could have been ours:
We are trapped under a weight of sin.
O Lord, we call to you:
forgive us and restore us,
through Jesus our redeemer. Amen.

7.29 CONFESSING OUR SINS

From 1 Corinthians 13

Let us confess our lack of love, and our need of grace:

Lord,
we have sometimes lost our patience,
we have been unkind,
we have been envious,
we have been rude and proud,
we have been selfish and irritable,
we have failed to forgive.
Have mercy on us, O God;

help us not to delight in evil,
but to rejoice in the truth;
help us always to protect, to trust,
    to hope and to persevere
until we see you face to face,
and learn to love as you love us;
in Jesus Christ our Lord. Amen.

7.30 CONFESSING OUR SINS

From Ephesians 5 and 6

(The bracketed section may be omitted)

O God, the Father of us all, we come to you in sorrow, for we have often failed you:

Lord, forgive us, and help us to obey.

You have taught us: 'Honour your father and mother, that it may go well with you and that you may enjoy long life on the earth.' We have often failed you:

Lord, forgive us, and help us to obey.

You have taught us as children: 'Obey your parents in the Lord, for this is right.' We have often failed you:

Lord, forgive us, and help us to obey.

You have taught us as fathers: 'Do not exasperate your children; instead, bring them up in the training and instruction of the Lord.' We have often failed you:

Lord, forgive us, and help us to obey.

You have taught us as mothers to live with sincere faith and bring our children to Christ. We have often failed you:

Lord, forgive us, and help us to obey.

[You have taught us as husbands: 'Love your wives as you love
yourselves.' We have often failed you:
Lord, forgive us, and help us to obey.

You have taught us as wives: 'Respect your husbands.' We have
often failed you:
Lord, forgive us, and help us to obey.]

You have taught us as the Christian family: 'Submit to one another
out of reverence for Christ.' We have often failed you:
Lord, forgive us, and help us to obey.

**Father, help us all to hear your word,
and to obey it; for Jesus' sake. Amen.**

7.31 CONFESSING OUR SINS
From 1 John 1
**O God,
you have taught us
that if we say we have no sin
we deceive ourselves
and the truth is not us:
we humbly confess our sins to you;
and we ask you to keep your promise
to forgive us our sins
and to cleanse us from all unrighteousness;
through Jesus Christ our Lord. Amen.**

7.32 CONFESSING OUR SINS AND DECLARING GOD'S FORGIVENESS

From 2 Samuel 12

Why have you rejected the word of the Lord by doing evil in his sight?

We have sinned against the Lord.

The Lord has taken away your sin; you will not die. **Amen.**

Declaring God's forgiveness

If we confess our sins, God is faithful and just and will forgive us our sins and purify us from all unrighteousness.

1 JOHN 1.9

8.1 DECLARING GOD'S FORGIVENESS
From Ezra 9
The Lord *your* God is gracious; he surrounds *you** with his love, gives light to *your* eyes and freedom from *your* sins. God has not deserted you – he shows *you* kindness and grants *you* new life; in Christ Jesus our Lord. **Amen.**

8.2 DECLARING GOD'S FORGIVENESS
From Nehemiah 9
The Lord our God is a forgiving God, gracious and merciful, slow to anger and full of love; because of his great compassion he will not abandon *you*. *You* were disobedient and rebelled against him, yet from heaven he hears *you* in *your* distress, he forgives *your* sin and delivers *you*; through Jesus Christ our Lord. **Amen.**

* words in italics may be changed to the first person (we, us, our, etc.)

8.3 DECLARING GOD'S FORGIVENESS

From Psalm 6

The Lord God be merciful to *you* and heal *you*; the Lord turn his face towards *you* and deliver *you*; the Lord save *you* in his unfailing love; through Jesus Christ. **Amen.**

8.4 DECLARING GOD'S FORGIVENESS

From Psalm 31

The Lord have mercy upon *you* in all *your* distress; the Lord deliver *you* from *your* sins and shelter *you* in all temptation; the Lord make his face to shine upon *you*, and save *you* in his unfailing love. **Amen.**

8.5 DECLARING GOD'S FORGIVENESS

From Psalm 32

You are blessed by the Lord: *your* sins are forgiven, *your* faults are covered; the Lord will not count *your* sin against *you*, for *you* have confessed to him and have not deceived him: [*let us*] rejoice in the Lord and be glad! **Amen.**

8.6 DECLARING GOD'S FORGIVENESS

From Psalm 51

The Lord your God loves *you* and has mercy on *you*; he forgives *your* waywardness and sin, he cleanses *your* heart and life and renews a right spirit within *you*; for Jesus' sake. **Amen.**

8.7 DECLARING GOD'S FORGIVENESS

From Psalm 51

God in his goodness have mercy on *you*, wash *you* clean from *your* guilt and purify *you* from *your* sin; God the righteous judge remove *your* sins from *you*, and make *you* whiter than snow; through Jesus Christ our Saviour. **Amen.**

8.8 DECLARING GOD'S FORGIVENESS
From Psalm 103 (variant)

The Lord forgives *you* all *your* sins, and heals the disease of *your* soul; the Lord redeems *your* life from the grave, and blesses *you* with his love and mercy. **Amen.**

8.9 DECLARING GOD'S FORGIVENESS
From Psalm 103

God who is merciful and loving will not punish *you* as you deserve, nor repay *you* for *your* sins and wrongdoing. As high as the sky is above the earth, so great is his love for *you*; as far as the east is from the west, so far has he removed *your* sins from *you*, through Jesus Christ our Lord. **Amen.**

8.10 DECLARING GOD'S FORGIVENESS
From Psalm 116

The Lord knows your voice, the Lord hears your cry for mercy, the Lord turns his ear toward you; the Lord is gracious and righteous, he is full of compassion. In your need he has saved you. (*Let us*) Be at peace – God forgives *you*. **Amen.**

8.11 DECLARING GOD'S FORGIVENESS
From Psalm 130

If God kept a record of your sins you could not stand; but with him there is forgiveness – therefore [let us] fear him, wait for him, put your hope in him. His love for you has not failed, and he has redeemed you from all your sins; through Christ, our Lord. **Amen.**

8.12 DECLARING GOD'S FORGIVENESS

From Psalm 130

O people, (*let us*) put *your* hope in the Lord:
his love will never fail us.

With the Lord there is full redemption:
he has redeemed us from all our sins.

8.13 DECLARING GOD'S FORGIVENESS

From Psalm 145

God is gracious and compassionate, slow to anger and rich in love;
he loves *you* and keeps his promise to forgive *you*; he lifts *you* up and
hears *your* cry and saves *you*, through Jesus Christ our Lord. **Amen.**

8.14 DECLARING GOD'S FORGIVENESS

From Isaiah 25

The faithful Lord, the sovereign Lord, wipes away *your* tears and
removes *your* disgrace from *you*. The Lord has spoken – he is *your*
God: trust him and he will save *you*, (*let us*) rejoice and be glad in
his redemption; through Christ Jesus. **Amen.**

8.15 DECLARING GOD'S FORGIVENESS

From Isaiah 38

The Lord restore *your* health, the Lord bring *you* salvation and let
you live; the Lord in his love keep *you* from destruction, and put
your sins behind his back for ever. **Amen.**

8.16 DECLARING GOD'S FORGIVENESS

From Isaiah 40

Hear God's tender words of comfort: 'Your struggles are over, your
sin is paid for'. God will show *you* his glory, and *you* will receive the
grace of forgiveness at his hand; in Jesus Christ, our Lord. **Amen.**

8.17 DECLARING GOD'S FORGIVENESS
From Isaiah 41
(*Let us*) receive forgiveness in the name of *your* God.

**We are God's servants –
he has chosen us and not rejected us:
we will not fear, for he is with us,
nor be afraid, for he is our God –
he will strengthen us and help us;
he will uphold us
      with his righteous right hand;
through Jesus Christ our Lord. Amen.**

8.18 DECLARING GOD'S FORGIVENESS
From Isaiah 43
The Lord *your* redeemer, the Holy One, blots out *your* transgressions and remembers *your* sins no more; for his name's sake. **Amen.**

8.19 DECLARING GOD'S FORGIVENESS
From Isaiah 53
Receive God's forgiveness through our Lord Jesus Christ: he covers *your* weaknesses and carries *your* sorrows; he was pierced for *your* transgressions and crushed for *your* iniquities; he took *your* punishment upon himself to bring *you* peace: by his wounds *you* are healed. **Amen.**

8.20 DECLARING GOD'S FORGIVENESS
From Isaiah 53
Like sheep *you* have gone astray, but the Lord has laid on Jesus the sins of us all. In Christ *you* are forgiven. **Amen.**

8.21 DECLARING GOD'S FORGIVENESS
From Isaiah 53
Jesus has taken *your* weaknesses and carried *your* sins; he has borne the punishment that brings *you* peace.
Thanks be to God. Amen.

8.22 DECLARING GOD'S FORGIVENESS
From Hosea 14
The Lord heals *your* waywardness and loves *you* freely; he is no longer angry with *you* and forgives *you*; through our Lord Jesus Christ. **Amen.**

8.23 DECLARING GOD'S FORGIVENESS
From Amos 5
(*Let us*) seek good and not evil and *you* shall live; hate evil, love good, and the Lord will be with *you*: God almighty has mercy upon *you*, through Jesus our redeemer. **Amen.**

8.24 DECLARING GOD'S FORGIVENESS
From 1 Corinthians 6
Now *you* are washed, *you* are sanctified, *you* are justified; in the name of the Lord Jesus and by the Spirit of our God. **Amen.**

8.25 DECLARING GOD'S FORGIVENESS
From Colossians 1
God has rescued *you* from the power of darkness, and brought *you* safe into the kingdom of his dear Son: in Christ *your* sins are forgiven, *you* are set free. **Amen.**

8.26 DECLARING GOD'S FORGIVENESS

From Hebrews 10

Draw near with a sincere heart and a sure faith: *you* are purged from *your* guilt and washed clean through the blood of Christ. (*Let us*) hold on to this hope, and trust the promises of God. **Amen.**

8.27 DECLARING GOD'S FORGIVENESS

From 1 John 4

Because God loves *you*, and by means of his Son whom God sent, *your* sins are forgiven. **Amen.**

8.28 DECLARING GOD'S FORGIVENESS

From Revelation 1

Jesus loves *you* and has saved *you* from *your* sins by his blood; he has made *you* to be a kingdom and priests to serve his God and Father:

to him be glory for ever and ever. Amen.

Receiving God's mercy

Lord, you have forgiven your people's sins and pardoned all their wrongs.

PSALM 85.2

_____

9.1 RECEIVING GOD'S MERCY
From Psalm 28
Let us praise the Lord,
for he has heard our cry for mercy:
in Christ we are forgiven,
he is our strength and shield –
let us trust in him and he will help us.
Let us rejoice and thank him in song,
for he is the strength of his people
and will be our salvation.
He will save us and bless us;
he will be our Shepherd
and care for us for ever. **Amen.**

9.2 RECEIVING GOD'S MERCY
From Psalm 99
The Lord our God answers our prayers and forgives our sins:
**let us praise our God,
for he is holy! Amen.**

9.3 RECEIVING GOD'S MERCY
From Isaiah 12
Surely God is my salvation;
I will trust and not be afraid.
The Lord, the Lord, is my strength and my song;
he has become my salvation. Amen.

9.4 RECEIVING GOD'S MERCY
From Isaiah 12
I praise you, O Lord:
although you were angry with me,
your anger has turned away
and you have comforted me. Amen.

9.5 RECEIVING GOD'S MERCY
From Isaiah 38
Lord, in your love
you kept me from the pit of destruction;
you have put all my sins behind your back. Amen.

9.6 RECEIVING GOD'S MERCY
From Ephesians 2
God's love for us is so great, and he is so rich in mercy that, even
when we were dead in our sins, he made us alive with Christ:
it is by God's grace we have been saved,
through faith.

This is not of yourselves – not the result of your own efforts:
it is the gift of God!

No one can boast about it:
it is by God's grace that we have been saved;
through Jesus Christ our Lord. Amen.

Proclaiming God's praise

I will proclaim the name of the Lord. O praise the greatness of our God!

DEUTERONOMY 32.3

It is good to praise the Lord and make music to your name, O Most High.

PSALM 92.1

10.1 PROCLAIMING GOD'S PRAISE

From Exodus 15

Let us sing to the Lord our God, majestic in holiness, awesome in glory, working wonders:

he is highly exalted,

and he will reign for ever and ever. Amen.

♪*

---

* The quaver sign indicates that the responsive item is suitable as an introduction to hymns or songs. When used in this way, the hymn or song should be announced before the response and the response should lead into the first line of the musical item.

10.2 PROCLAIMING GOD'S PRAISE

From Exodus 15

The Lord is my strength and my song:
he has become my salvation.

He is the God of my ancestors, and I will exalt him:
he is my God and I will praise him.

10.3 PROCLAIMING GOD'S PRAISE

From Deuteronomy 32

Let us proclaim the name of the Lord:
O, praise the greatness of our God!
♪

10.4 PROCLAIMING GOD'S PRAISE

From Psalm 27

In God's sanctuary bring your sacrifice of praise with shouts of joy:
we will sing and make music to the Lord.

O Lord, hear our voices when we call – be merciful and answer as
we seek his face:
your face, Lord, we will seek. Amen.

10.5 PROCLAIMING GOD'S PRAISE

From Psalm 30

Sing praise to the Lord, all his faithful people; remember what the
Holy One has done and give him thanks! **Amen.**
♪

10.6 PROCLAIMING GOD'S PRAISE
From Psalm 30
Sing to the Lord, you saints of the Lord:
praise his holy name!
♪

10.7 PROCLAIMING GOD'S PRAISE
From Psalm 34
Glorify the Lord with me:
let us praise his name together. Amen.
♪

10.8 PROCLAIMING GOD'S PRAISE
From Psalm 66
Shout with joy to God, all the earth:
sing to the glory of his name.

Come and see what God has done:
how awesome are his works!

Praise our God, all you people:
sound aloud his praise. Amen.
♪

10.9 PROCLAIMING GOD'S PRAISE
From Psalm 72
Praise to the Lord, our God:
praise his glorious name for ever.

Let the earth be filled with his glory:
Amen. Amen.
♪

10.10 PROCLAIMING GOD'S PRAISE
From Psalm 72
Praise the Lord, the God of Israel:
he alone does marvellous things.

Praise his glorious name for ever:
let his praises fill the earth!
♪

10.11 PROCLAIMING GOD'S PRAISE
From Psalm 89
Sing for ever of the love of the Lord; let every generation declare
his praise:
Lord, your love stands firm for ever,
your faithfulness is mirrored in the skies;
in your name we rejoice,
in your truth we exult.

Praise the Lord:
hallelujah. Amen.
♪

10.12 PROCLAIMING GOD'S PRAISE
From Psalm 95
Sing for joy to the Lord:
shout to the Rock of our salvation.

Come before him with thanksgiving:
sing him joyful songs of praise! Amen.
♪

10.13 PROCLAIMING GOD'S PRAISE

From Psalm 103

Praise the Lord, O my soul:
all my being, praise his name!

Praise the Lord, O my soul:
and forget not all his blessings!

Praise the Lord, O my soul:
Praise the Lord! Amen.
♪

OR

10.14 PROCLAIMING GOD'S PRAISE

From Psalm 103

Praise the Lord, O my soul:
all my being,
praise his holy name.

Praise the Lord, O my soul:
never forget his blessings. Amen.

10.15 PROCLAIMING GOD'S PRAISE

From Psalm 113

Praise the Lord, you servants of the Lord:
Praise his name!

His name be praised, now and for ever:
From the east to the west
praise the name of the Lord!
♪

10.16 PROCLAIMING GOD'S PRAISE

From Psalm 138

Praise the Lord with all your heart:
O Lord, we sing your praise,
we bow down in your presence.

Lord, we praise you for your love and faithfulness:
your name and your word are exalted above all things;
your love, O Lord, endures for ever. Amen.
♪

10.17 PROCLAIMING GOD'S PRAISE

From Isaiah 12

Sing to the Lord:
he has done glorious things.

Let this be known in all the world. **Amen.**
♪

10.18 PROCLAIMING GOD'S PRAISE

From Isaiah 12

People of our God, shout aloud and sing for joy:
great is the Holy One among us! Amen.
♪

10.19 PROCLAIMING GOD'S PRAISE

From Isaiah 12

Give thanks to the Lord, call on his name; make known among the
nations what he has done:
his name is exalted for ever. Amen.

10.20 PROCLAIMING GOD'S PRAISE

From Isaiah 23 and 24

Lord Almighty, you bring low all pride and glory, you humble the famous in the earth; you stretch out your hand over the sea and make the nations tremble. To you we raise our voices, and shout for joy; we acclaim your majesty, we give you praise, we exalt your name. From the ends of the earth we proclaim:

Glory to the righteous One,

who reigns among us for ever and ever! Amen.

10.21 PROCLAIMING GOD'S PRAISE

From Isaiah 25

O Lord, we exalt and praise your name, for you are faithful to us and have done marvellous things – things promised long ago:

you are our God –

we trust in you, and you save us;

through Jesus our redeemer. Amen.

10.22 PROCLAIMING GOD'S PRAISE

From Isaiah 42

Sing to the Lord a new song:

praise God, all the world!

♪

10.23 PROCLAIMING GOD'S PRAISE

From Philippians 4

Sisters and brothers, rejoice in the Lord! **Amen.**

♪

10.24 PROCLAIMING GOD'S PRAISE
From Philippians 4
Rejoice in the Lord always:
rejoice in the Lord –
hallelujah! Amen.
♪

10.25 PROCLAIMING GOD'S PRAISE
From 1 Peter 2
We are a chosen people, a royal priesthood, a holy nation, a people
belonging to God:
let us declare God's praises,
who calls us out of darkness
into his marvellous light!
♪

10.26 PROCLAIMING GOD'S PRAISE
From Revelation 19
Praise God!
The Lord our almighty God is king!

Rejoice and be glad:
praise his greatness! Amen.
♪

Saying a psalm together

Speak to one another with the words of psalms, hymns, and sacred songs;
sing hymns and psalms to the Lord with praise in your hearts.

EPHESIANS 5.19

11.1 SAYING A PSALM TOGETHER
From Psalm 1
Happy are those who do not take the advice of the wicked:
or follow the path of sinners,
or sit in the seat of scoffers.

Happy are those who delight in the law of the Lord:
who think about it day and night.

Like a tree planted by the waterside, they bear fruit in due time and
their leaves do not wither:
they prosper in all they do.

The wicked are different:
they are like chaff;
the wind blows them away.

The wicked cannot stand up to God's judgement:
sinners cannot worship with the righteous.

The Lord God watches over the righteous; and the wicked perish.
[Amen.

Glory be to God,
Father, Son and Holy Spirit,
for ever. Amen.]*

* Inclusion of text within square brackets will be a matter of local choice.

11.8* SAYING A PSALM TOGETHER

From Psalm 8

Part options: the congregation may divide at 'A', 'B', and 'C'

O Lord, our Lord:

how great is your name in all the world!

A **Your glory fills the skies;**

B **your praise is sung by children;**

C **you silence your enemies.**

I look at the universe your hands have made, the moon and the stars you put in place:

ALL **Who are we that you care for us?**

You made us less than gods:

ALL **you crowned us with glory and honour.**

You put us in charge of creation:

A **the beasts of the field.**

B **the birds of the air.**

C **the fish of the sea.**

O Lord, our Lord:

ALL **how great is your name in all the world! [Amen.**

Glory be to God,
Father, Son and Holy Spirit,
for ever. Amen.]

*Items in this chapter are numbered according to the psalm from which they derive.

11.15 SAYING A PSALM TOGETHER
From Psalm 15

Lord, who may come into your holy place:
who may live in your presence?

Lord, we may live in your presence:
if our way is blameless,
if we do what is righteous,
if we speak the truth from our heart.

Lord, we may live in your presence:
if we do not tell lies;
if we do not slander our neighbours,
if we do not despise others.

Lord, we may live in your presence:
if we shun the wicked,
if we honour the godly,
if we keep our promises, even when it hurts.

Lord, we may live in your presence:
if we lend money without exacting interest,
if we refuse to be bribed,
if we protect the innocent.

If we do these things:
we will never be dismayed. [Amen.

Glory be to God,
Father, Son and Holy Spirit,
for ever. Amen.]

11.19 SAYING A PSALM TOGETHER

From Psalm 19

We see God's glory in the heavens:
the skies proclaim his skill.

Day after day, night after night: we see his wisdom on display:
all without voice or speech –
we hear no sound!

There is no language in which they cannot be understood:
yet their message reaches the ends of the earth.

Like a bridegroom arriving, like a champion athlete enjoying the
race, is the sun God has placed in the heavens; we see it rise in
the east.
We see it set in the west:
nothing can be hidden from its heat.

God's law is perfect:
it renews our strength

God's commandments are trustworthy:
they make the simple wise.

God's rules are right:
they bring joy to the heart.

God's insights are true:
they bring light to the eyes.

God's reign is holy:
it lasts for ever.

God's words are reliable:
they are absolutely right.

They are more precious than gold:
sweeter than honey.

Lord, all these are for our warning:
and for our reward when we obey you.

Rarely can we see our own failings:
Lord, forgive me for my hidden faults.

Free me from deliberate sins:
do not let them get a hold over me.

Lord, free me from the evil of sin:
make me holy.

O Lord, my refuge and my redeemer:
let my thoughts and my words
always be acceptable to you. [Amen.

Glory be to God,
Father, Son and Holy Spirit,
for ever. Amen.]

11.21 SAYING A PSALM TOGETHER
From Psalm 21
Lord, we rejoice in your strength:
we exalt in your victory.

You have granted our heart's desire:
you have not rejected our prayers.

You favour us with blessing and peace:
you crown us with loving-kindness.

We asked you for life:
you gave us eternal life.

Your victory has brought us to glory:
we rejoice in your presence for ever.

We place ourselves in your loving care:
we shall never be removed.

Receive our song, a psalm of praise:
be exalted, O Lord, our God. [Amen.

Glory be to God,
Father, Son and Holy Spirit,
for ever. Amen.]

11.22 SAYING A PSALM TOGETHER
From Psalm 22

O God, my God, why have you forsaken me?
Why do you seem so far away,
why don't you save me,
why don't you hear me crying?

Yet you are the Holy One:
you are enthroned
amid the praises of your people.

Our ancestors put their faith in you:
you rescued them.

They cried out to you:
you saved them.

They trusted you:
you did not disappoint them.

But I am a worm – a nobody; people scorn me, they despise me:
everyone who sees me mocks me;
they all slander me, shaking their heads.

He trusts in the Lord, let the Lord rescue him!
Let God save him,
since he loves him!

Yet, you gave me birth:
you made me trust you.

I have always loved you:
do not be far away,
for troubles are near,
and no one else can save.

[Glory be to God,
Father, Son and Holy Spirit,
for ever. Amen.]

11.23 SAYING A PSALM TOGETHER
From Psalm 23
The Lord is my shepherd:
I shall not lack for anything.

He makes me lie down in green pastures:
he leads me beside still waters.

He refreshes my soul:
he guides me along paths of righteousness;
for his name's sake.

Even though I walk through shadows in the darkest valley:
I will fear no evil, for you are with me.
your rod and your staff – they comfort me.

You have set a table before me where my enemies surround me:
you anoint my head with oil –
my cup overflows.

Surely goodness and love will follow me all the days of my life:
and I will live in the presence of the Lord for ever. [Amen.

Glory be to God,
Father, Son and Holy Spirit,
for ever. Amen.]

11.24 SAYING A PSALM TOGETHER
From Psalm 24
Part options: 'E' – enquirer; 'D' – director; or these lines may also be said
by the minister/leader.
The earth is the Lord's, and everything in it:
the world, and all who live here.

He founded it upon the seas:
and established it upon the waters.

ᴱ Who has the right to go up the Lord's hill; who may enter his holy
temple?
**Those who have clean hands
and a pure heart,
who do not worship idols
or swear by what is false.**

They receive blessing continually from the Lord:
and righteousness from the God of their salvation.

Such are the people who seek for God;
who enter the presence of the God of Jacob.

ᴰ Fling wide the gates, open the ancient doors:
that the king of glory may come in.

ᴱ Who is the king of glory?
The Lord, strong and mighty, the Lord mighty in battle.

ᴰ Fling wide the gates, open the ancient doors:
that the king of glory may come in.

ᴱ Who is he, this king of glory?
**The Lord almighty,
he is the king of glory.**

[**Glory be to God,
Father, Son and Holy Spirit,
for ever. Amen.**]

11.27 SAYING A PSALM TOGETHER
From Psalm 27
The Lord is my light and my salvation:
whom should I fear?

The Lord is the refuge of my life:
of whom should I be afraid?

When those who would do me harm come near to consume me, it
is they who stumble and fall:
If an army came against me
I would not need to fear.

The only things I ask from the Lord are these:
to live in God's presence all the days of my life;
to see his beauty and to worship him.

Hear me, O Lord, when I call to you:
have mercy, Lord, and answer me.

Come into the presence of the Lord:
I come to find you, Lord,
do not hide your face from me.

Lord, do not turn away from me in your anger, for you have always
been my help:
God, my Saviour,
do not leave me –
do not reject me.

Though my mother and my father leave me, the Lord will look
after me:
**I know that I shall see the goodness of the Lord
in the land of the living.**

Wait for the Lord, be strong and courageous, put your hope in
the Lord:
Amen.

**Glory be to God,
Father, Son and Holy Spirit,
for ever. Amen.**

11.33 SAYING A PSALM TOGETHER
From Psalm 33
Sing joyfully to the Lord, you righteous:
it is right that his people should praise him.

Praise the Lord with the harp:
make music to him on the strings.

Sing to the Lord a new song:
play skilfully, and shout for joy.

For the word of the Lord is right and true:
and all his work is faithfulness.

The Lord loves righteousness and justice:
his endless love fills the earth.

By the word of the Lord the universe was formed:
his breath created moon and stars.

Let all the earth fear the Lord:
the people of the world revere him.

For he spoke, and it came to be:
he commanded, and all was made.

The Lord frustrates the nations:
he brings their councils to nothing.

God's purposes are sure:
his plans endure for ever.

Happy is the nation whose God is the Lord:
happy the people he makes his own.

The eyes of the Lord are on those who fear him:
who trust in his unfailing love.

We wait in hope for the Lord:
he is our help and shield.

In him our hearts rejoice:
we trust his holy name.

May your constant love be with us, Lord:
as we put our hope in you. [Amen.

**Glory be to God,
Father, Son and Holy Spirit,
for ever. Amen.]**

11.36 SAYING A PSALM TOGETHER
From Psalm 36
O Lord, your goodness reaches the heavens:
your faithfulness extends to the skies.

Your righteousness is like the towering mountains:
your justice is like the great deep.

How precious is your goodness, O God:
we find shelter under your wings!

We feast on the food you provide:
we drink from the river of your goodness.

For with you is the fountain of life:
in your light we see light. [Amen.

**Glory be to God,
Father, Son and Holy Spirit,
for ever. Amen.]**

11.40 SAYING A PSALM TOGETHER
From Psalm 40
I waited patiently for the Lord:
he turned and heard my cry.

He lifted me out of the slimy pit:
out of the mud and mire.

He set my feet upon the rock:
he gave me a place to stand.

He put a new song in my mouth –
a hymn of praise to God.

Many will see it and fear:
and put their trust in the Lord. [Amen.

Glory be to God,
Father, Son and Holy Spirit,
for ever. Amen.]

11.41 SAYING A PSALM TOGETHER
From Psalm 41
Blessing be upon you when you care for the weak; the Lord deliver
you in your time of trouble:
    the Lord protect you and preserve you,
    the Lord bless you where you live,
    the Lord defend you from adversity,
    the Lord support you in sickness and in health,
    the Lord restore your life. **Amen.**

O Lord, have mercy on me,
for I have sinned against you;
I have suffered the malice of my enemies
and the opposition of my closest friends –
but you, O Lord, uphold me in innocence;
keep me in your presence for ever. Amen.

Praise be to the Lord; the God of Israel, from everlasting to everlasting:
Amen and amen.

[Glory be to God,
Father, Son and Holy Spirit,
for ever. Amen.]

11.42 SAYING A PSALM TOGETHER
From Psalm 42

As the deer thirsts for running water:
so I long for you, O God.

I thirst for God, the living God:
when shall I come into your presence?

I survive on tears day and night, and everyone asks me:
'Where is your God now?'

As I pour out my soul I remember how I used to go ahead of the
crowd – the festival pilgrims – to the Lord's house, joining in the
shouts of praise.
why am I so dejected;
why groaning in my heart?

Put your trust in God: go on praising him – he will yet deliver you:
I have experienced the depths of sorrow,
I have heard the sound of waves sweeping over me.

Yet by day the Lord continues his love to me, by night his praise is
on my lips:
I pray to the God of my life.

I say to God my rock:
why have you forgotten me?

Why must I go about mourning:
why endure the taunts of the enemy?

My enemy taunts me all day long:
'Where is your God now?'

Why are you so dejected, why groaning in your heart – put your
trust in God:
I will go on praising him,
for he will yet deliver me. [Amen.

Glory be to God,
Father, Son and Holy Spirit,
for ever. Amen.]

11.51 SAYING A PSALM TOGETHER
From Psalms 51 and 143 (adapted for use together, with the Holy Spirit as
the theme)
O Lord, I spread my hands out to you:
I thirst for you like dry ground.

Teach me to do your will, for you are my God:
let your good Spirit lead me in safety.

You require sincerity and truth in me:
fill my mind with wisdom.

Create in me a pure heart, O God:
and renew a faithful spirit in me.

Do not cast me from your presence:
or take your Holy Spirit from me.

Give me again the joy of your salvation:
and make me willing to obey. [Amen.

Glory be to God,
Father, Son and Holy Spirit,
for ever. Amen.]

11.65 SAYING A PSALM TOGETHER

From Psalm 65

O God, it is right for us to praise you:
you are the one who answers our prayers.

You care for the land and water it:
you make it rich and fertile.

You fill the running streams with water:
you irrigate the land.

You soften the ground with showers:
you make the young crops grow.

You crown the year with your goodness:
you give us a plentiful harvest.

The pastures are filled with flocks:
the hillsides are clothed with joy.

The fields are covered with grain:
they shout for joy and sing. [Amen.

Glory be to God,
Father, Son and Holy Spirit,
for ever. Amen.]

11.67 SAYING A PSALM TOGETHER
From Psalm 67
O God, be gracious to us and bless us:
make your face to shine upon us.

Let your ways be known upon earth:
your saving grace to every nation.

Let the peoples praise you, O God:
let all the peoples praise you.

Let the nations be glad:
and sing aloud for joy.

Because you judge the peoples justly:
and guide the nations of the earth.

Let the peoples praise you, O God:
let all the peoples praise you.

Then the land will yield his harvest:
God, our God, will bless us.

God will bless us:
and all the world will fear him. [Amen.

**Glory be to God,
Father, Son and Holy Spirit,
for ever. Amen.]**

11.84 SAYING A PSALM TOGETHER
From Psalm 84

O Lord almighty, my king and my God:
how lovely is your dwelling-place!

I long to be in your presence:
my soul cries out for the living God.

O Lord almighty, my king and my God, the sparrow may find a
home in your sanctuary, the swallow may make a nest to rear
beside your altar to rear her young: happy are those who dwell in
your house:
they need never stop praising you!

Happy are the pilgrims who come to your house:
they find their strength in your presence!

As they pass through the dry valley:
it becomes for them a place of springs.

So they enter through the walls:
and come into the presence of God.

[O Lord almighty,
hear our prayer.
God save the *Queen*, the one you have anointed.]

One day in your presence is better than a thousand anywhere else:
better to stand at the door of your house,
than to live in the ways of ungodliness.

The Lord God be your sun and your shield; the Lord withhold no good thing from you as you walk before him in innocence. **Amen.**

O Lord, almighty,
happy are those who trust in you.

[Glory be to God,
Father, Son and Holy Spirit,
for ever. Amen.]

11.89 SAYING A PSALM TOGETHER

From Psalm 89

Sing for ever of the love of the Lord; let every generation declare his praise:
Lord, your love stands firm for ever:
your faithfulness is mirrored in the skies –
let the heavens praise your wonders,
let angels proclaim your faithfulness!

Who is like the Lord?
Lord, there is no one like you –
you rule the raging sea,
you calm the rising waves.
The heavens are yours,
the earth is yours,
and all that lives upon the earth is yours.

Who is like the Lord?
Lord, there is no one like you –
your sceptre is righteousness,
your throne is justice,
your heralds are love and faithfulness.

Happy are those who come to praise you, for they will walk in the
light of your presence:
in your name we rejoice,
in your truth we exult.

You are the strength of your people, and their glory:
because of your love we can hold our heads up high!

Praise the Lord for ever and ever:
Amen and amen!

[Glory be to God,
Father, Son and Holy Spirit,
for ever. Amen.]

11.90 SAYING A PSALM TOGETHER

From Psalm 90
Lord, you have been our refuge:
through every generation.

Before the mountains came to be, before the earth was born:
from everlasting to everlasting you are God.

You turn everyone to dust; 'Return to dust', you say:
A thousand years in your sight
is merely like a day passing;
like a brief moment in the night.

You sweep away everyone into the sleep of death:
we fade like flowers –
fresh in the morning,
dry and withered in the evening.

Lord, we are consumed by your anger, terrified by your indignation:
you expose our sins,
our secret sins,
in the light of your being.

All our days are overshadowed by your wrath:
they end like a sigh.

We only live for seventy years – eighty if we are strong. The years
bring hard work and trouble; they fly past and we are soon
forgotten:
teach us to value our days,
make our heart wise.

Lord, how long will our troubles last?
Have mercy on your servants;
satisfy us in the morning with your unfailing love,
that we may rejoice and be glad all our days.

Lord, restore days of happiness for our days of suffering, years of
joy for our years of trouble:
Lord, show your saving power to your servants
and your glory to our children.

The favour of the Lord our God rest upon *you*; the Lord establish
the work of *your* hands: [**Amen.**

Glory be to God,
Father, Son and Holy Spirit,
for ever. Amen.]

11.91 SAYING A PSALM TOGETHER

From Psalm 91

Part options: 'G' – the voice of God (voice only)

All who live in the shelter of the Most High, who rest in the shade
of the almighty – proclaim him!
He is our refuge and our rock;
he is our God –
in him we trust.

He will rescue you from snares and perils:
he will cover us with his wings,
we will find refuge beneath his care.

His faithfulness is your shield and defence:
we will not fear the terror of the night
or the perils of the day –
O God, you are our refuge.

All who live in the presence of the Most High, no disaster will stalk
you, no calamity will befall your home:
he will command his angels to watch over us wherever we go.

G Because you love me, I will rescue you, I will set you free; because
you know my name I will lift you to safety.
when I call to God he will answer,
he will be with me in time of trouble,
he will rescue me and guard my honour,
he will satisfy me all my life long –
and then I shall see his salvation. Amen.

[Glory be to God,
Father, Son and Holy Spirit,
for ever. Amen.]

11.93 SAYING A PSALM TOGETHER

From Psalm 93

The Lord reigns, robed in majesty:
he arms himself with power.

The earth is firmly set in place:
it can never be moved.

Your throne was founded long ago:
before all time began.

The oceans raise their voice, O Lord:
and lift their roaring waves.

The Lord is mightier than the sea:
he rules supreme on high.

O Lord our God, your laws stand firm through endless days:
your praise for evermore. [Amen.

Glory be to God,
Father, Son and Holy Spirit,
for ever. Amen.]

11.95 SAYING A PSALM TOGETHER

From Psalm 95

Part options: 'M' – first minister/leader; 'N' – second minister/leader;
'G' – voice (only) of God

ᴹ Come, let us joyfully praise our God, acclaiming the Rock of our salvation;

ᴺ come before him with thanksgiving, and greet him with melody:
our God is a great God –
a king above all other gods.

ᴹ The depths of the earth are in his hands:
ᴺ **the mountain peaks belong to him.**

The sea is his – he made it;
his own hands prepared the land.

ᴹ Come, bow down to worship God;
ᴺ kneel before the Lord who made us:
we are his people, the sheep of his flock.

ᴹ If you hear his voice today, do not harden your heart as his people did at Meribah – on that day at Massah in the desert:

ᴳ There they tested me and tried me even though they had seen what I did; for forty years I was angry with their generation – a people whose hearts went astray and did not follow my ways. I swore in my anger, 'They shall not enter my rest'.

ᴹ Come, bow down to worship God;
ᴺ kneel before the Lord who made us:
Amen. Amen.

[**Glory be to God,
Father, Son and Holy Spirit,
for ever. Amen.**]

11.96 SAYING A PSALM TOGETHER
From Psalm 96

Sing to the Lord a new song:
sing to the Lord, all the earth.

Sing to the Lord, praise his name:
proclaim his salvation each day.

Declare his glory among the nations:
his marvellous deeds among the peoples.

Great is the Lord, and worthy of praise:
honour him above all gods.

Splendour and majesty surround him:
power and beauty fill his temple.

Praise the Lord all people on earth:
praise his glory and might.

Give him the glory due to his name:
bring an offering into his temple.

Worship the Lord in his beauty and holiness:
tremble before him all the earth.

Say to the nations:
The Lord is king!

Let the heavens rejoice and the earth be glad:
let all creation sing for joy.

For God shall come to judge the world:
and rule the people with his truth.
[Amen.

Glory be to God,
Father, Son and Holy Spirit,
for ever. Amen.]

11.98 SAYING A PSALM TOGETHER
From Psalm 95 (Short rhythmic version)
Sing to the Lord a new song:
for he has done marvellous things.

His right hand and his holy arm:
have brought a great triumph to us.

He lets his salvation be known:
his righteousness seen by the world.

His glory is witnessed by all:
to us he continues his love.

Rejoice in the Lord, all the earth:
burst into jubilant song.

Make music to God with the harp:
with songs and the sound of your praise.

Sing praises to God as your king:
with trumpets and blast of the horn.

Let rivers and streams clap their hands:
the mountains together sing praise.

The Lord comes to judge the whole earth:
in righteousness God rules the world.
[Amen.

Glory be to God,
Father, Son and Holy Spirit,
for ever. Amen.]

11.99 SAYING A PSALM TOGETHER
From Psalm 99
Part options: the congregation may divide at 'A' and 'B'
The Lord reigns:
^ **let the nations tremble!**

He sits enthroned on high:
ᴮ **let the earth shake!**

Great is the Lord our God:
^ **exalted over all the world.**

Let the nations praise his awesome name, and say:
^ **God is holy!**

Praise the Lord and worship at his feet:
ᴮ **God is holy!**

Exalt the Lord your God, and worship on his holy mountain:
ᴬᴸᴸ **The Lord our God is holy!**

[Glory be to God,
Father, Son and Holy Spirit,
for ever. Amen.]

11.100 SAYING A PSALM TOGETHER

From Psalm 100

Rejoice in the Lord, all the earth:
worship the Lord with gladness.

Remember, the Lord is our God:
we are his flock and he made us.

Come to his temple with praise:
enter his gates with thanksgiving.

Thank him, sing praise to his name
good to us all is the Lord!

The love of the Lord will not fail:
God will be faithful for ever.

**[Glory be to God,
Father, Son and Holy Spirit,
for ever. Amen.]**

11.104 SAYING A PSALM TOGETHER
From Psalm 104 (Shortened version)
O Lord our God, you are very great:
you are clothed in splendour and majesty.

You make winds your messengers:
and flashes of fire your servants.

How many are your works:
the earth is full of your creatures!

When you hide your face, they are afraid:
when you take away their breath, they die.

When you send your Spirit they are created:
and you renew the face of the earth. [Amen.

Glory be to God,
Father, Son and Holy Spirit,
for ever. Amen.]

11.119(33) SAYING A PSALM TOGETHER
From Psalm 119 (beginning verse 33)

O Lord, teach me your commandments:
I want to follow them always.

Give me the wisdom to keep your law:
to obey it with all my heart.

Make me walk in the paths of your instruction:
there I shall find delight.

Turn my heart towards your teaching:
and away from my selfishness.

Turn my eyes away from all that is wrong:
speak to me and give me life.

Fulfil in me your promise:
your promise for those who fear you.

Let me not fall into the disgrace I fear:
but instead live by your truth.

How I long for your word!
In your righteousness, grant me life. [Amen.

Glory be to God,
Father, Son and Holy Spirit,
for ever. Amen.]

11.119(145) SAYING A PSALM TOGETHER
From Psalm 119 (beginning verse 145)

O Lord, my heart cries out to you:
answer me, and I will obey you.

I call to you, O Lord:
save me,
and I will keep your commandments.

Before the dawn breaks I rise and call on you to help me:
I have trusted in your word.

My eyes stay open during the long hours of the night:
that I may think about your promises.

Lord, as you love me hear my prayer:
save my life, O Lord,
as you have promised.

Those who scheme wickedly have come close to me, Lord, but they
are far from your commandments:
yet you are near me, Lord,
and all your commandments are true.

Long ago I learned that your laws last for ever. [**Amen.**

Glory be to God,
Father, Son and Holy Spirit,
for ever. Amen.]

11.119(169) SAYING A PSALM TOGETHER
From Psalm 119 (beginning verse 169)

O Lord, hear the cry of my heart:
give me understanding as you have promised:

Receive my prayers:
be true to your promise, and save me.

Let my lips overflow with praises as you teach me your decrees:
let my tongue sing of your word –
all your commandments are just.

Let your hand be upon me, O Lord:
I have chosen to follow your way.

I long for your salvation, Lord:
your law is my delight.

Give me life in which to praise you:
and instruction for my help.

Lord, I have strayed like a lost sheep:
come to search for me –
for I have not forgotten your commandments. [Amen.

Glory be to God,
Father, Son and Holy Spirit,
for ever. Amen.]

11.121 SAYING A PSALM TOGETHER

From Psalm 121

When I lift up my eyes to the hills, where do I find help?
My help comes only from the Lord,
the creator of heaven and earth.

He will not let you stumble; he who cares for you will not fall asleep:
the guardian of Israel will never slumber or sleep.

The Lord watches over you; the Lord stands at your right hand and
casts his shadow over you:
the sun will not strike you by day
or the moon by night.

The Lord keep you from all harm, the Lord guard your life, the
Lord watch over you as you come and go:
now and for ever. [Amen.

Glory be to God,
Father, Son and Holy Spirit,
for ever. Amen.]

11.122 SAYING A PSALM TOGETHER

From Psalm 122 (Abbreviated version)

I was glad when they said to me:
let us go to the house of the Lord!

Pray for the peace of Jerusalem:
may those who love our land be blessed.

May there be peace in your homes, salvation for your families:
for the sake of those we love we say –
Let there be peace! [Amen.

Glory be to God,
Father, Son and Holy Spirit,
for ever. Amen.]

11.126 SAYING A PSALM TOGETHER

From Psalm 126

When the Lord brought us back from slavery:
we were like those who dream.

Our mouths were filled with laughter:
our tongues with songs of joy.

Then those around us said, 'The Lord has done great things for
them':
The Lord has done great things for us,
and we are filled with joy.

Lord, like streams in the desert:
so restore our fortunes.

Those who go out in tears with seed to sow:
shall come back with their sheaves,
rejoicing! [Amen.

Glory be to God,
Father, Son and Holy Spirit,
for ever. Amen.]

11.128 SAYING A PSALM TOGETHER

From Psalm 128

Part options: 'P' – pilgrim, 'M' – minister

ᴹ The pilgrims' song:

ᴀʟʟ **blessed are those who fear the Lord,
who walk in his ways.**

ᴹ You will enjoy the fruit of your work; blessings and prosperity will be yours:

**blessed are those who fear the Lord,
who walk in his ways.**

ᴾ Your wife will be like a fruitful vine within your house; your children will be like young olive trees around your table:

ᴀʟʟ **blessed are those who fear the Lord,
who walk in his ways.**

ᴹ The Lord bless you all the days of your life; may you have prosperity; may you live to see your children's children:

ᴾ **Peace be with you.**

ᴀʟʟ **[Amen.**

**Glory be to God,
Father, Son and Holy Spirit,
for ever. Amen.]**

11.131 SAYING A PSALM TOGETHER
From Psalm 131

O Lord, do not let my heart be proud:
do not let my eyes be haughty.

I will not concern myself with lofty ideas:
or things that are beyond me.

My spirit shall be still, like a child asleep in the arms of its mother:
like a child asleep in its mother's arms.

O people, put your trust in the Lord:
from this time on,
for evermore! [Amen.

Glory be to God,
Father, Son and Holy Spirit,
for ever. Amen.]

11.139 SAYING A PSALM TOGETHER
From Psalm 139

Lord, you have searched my heart – and you know me:
you know me when I am resting,
you know me when I am working;
you know my thoughts from far away.

You know where I go and where I stay:
you know all the paths I tread.

Even before I have spoken a word, you know all about it:
you are my shield
behind me and in front of me,
your hand is laid upon me.

Such wonderful knowledge is beyond my understanding:
so high I cannot reach it.

Lord, where can I hide from your spirit?
Where can I run from your presence?

If I climb up to the skies, you are there:
if I descend to the depths you are there.

If I travel east where the sun rises, you are there:
if I sail west across the sea you are there.

With one hand you made me:
with the other you protect me.

If I say, 'Surely the darkness will hide me; the day will turn to night
around me.'
darkness is not dark for you,
and night is bright as day!

You created all of me, you formed me in my mother's womb:
I praise you Lord,
for you made me and you know me;
all you do is wonderful.

O God,
test me, and know my mind,
understand my anxious thoughts;
keep me from any path that grieves you,
and lead me in the way everlasting. [Amen.

Glory be to God,
Father, Son and Holy Spirit,
for ever. Amen.]

11.148 SAYING A PSALM TOGETHER

From Psalm 148

Part options: the congregation may divide at 'A' and 'B'

Praise the Lord!

Praise the Lord from the heavens:
praise him in the heights above.

Praise him, all his angels:
ᴬ **praise him, all his heavenly host.**

Praise him, sun and moon:
ᴮ **praise him, all you shining stars.**

Let them praise the name of the Lord:
ᴬᴸᴸ **Praise the Lord!**

Praise the Lord from the earth:
ᴬ **praise him, great sea creatures.**

Praise him, storms and clouds:
ᴮ **praise him, mountains and hills.**

Praise him, fields and woods:
ᴬ **praise him, animals and birds.**

Praise him, rulers and nations:
ᴮ **praise him, old and young.**

Let them praise the name of the Lord:
ᴬᴸᴸ **Praise the Lord! Amen.**

[**Glory be to God,**
Father, Son and Holy Spirit,
for ever. Amen.]

12

Reading from the Bible

Ezra read the Law to the people, and they all listened attentively. He stood on the platform high above the people, they all kept their eyes fixed on him. As soon as he opened the book, they all stood up.

NEHEMIAH 8.1–5

_____

All Scripture is inspired by God and is useful for teaching the truth, rebuking error, correcting faults, and giving instruction for right living.

2 TIMOTHY 3.16

_____

12.1 READING FROM THE BIBLE
From Exodus 24, after a reading
This is the book of the Covenant:
**everything the Lord has commanded
we will obey.**

OR

12.2 READING FROM THE BIBLE
From Exodus 24, after a reading
These are the Lord's words and laws:
everything the Lord has said we will do.

12.3 READING FROM THE BIBLE
From Deuteronomy 8, Matthew 4, Luke 4, after a reading
We cannot live on bread alone:
but by every word
that comes from the mouth of God.

12.4 READING FROM THE BIBLE
From 2 Samuel 22, after a reading
You are our lamp, O Lord:
you turn our darkness into light. Amen.

12.5 READING FROM THE BIBLE
From 1 Kings 22, after a reading
Let God's people mark these words:
the Lord has spoken. Amen.

12.6 READING FROM THE BIBLE
From Nehemiah 8, before a reading
Praise the Lord, the great God:
Amen. Amen.

12.7 READING FROM THE BIBLE
From Psalm 130, before a reading
We wait eagerly for the Lord:
in his word we trust.

12.8 READING FROM THE BIBLE
From Isaiah 25, after a first reading
This is our God:
we trust in him and he saves us.

12.9 READING FROM THE BIBLE

From Isaiah 25, after a second reading

This is the Lord:

let us rejoice and be glad in his salvation.

12.10 READING FROM THE BIBLE

From Jeremiah 9, before a reading

Let us hear God's word:

let us listen to the Lord.

12.11 READING FROM THE BIBLE

From Mark 4, after a reading

Those who have a mind to hear, let them hear! **Amen.**

12.12 READING FROM THE BIBLE

From 1 Peter 1, after a first reading

The word of the Lord remains for ever. **Amen.**

12.13 READING FROM THE BIBLE

From 1 Peter 1, after a Gospel reading

This is the Gospel we proclaim. **Amen.**

12.14 READING FROM THE BIBLE

From Revelation 1, before or after a reading

Blest is the one who reads these words:

**blest are those who hear them
and take to heart what is written.**

12.15 READING FROM THE BIBLE
From Revelation 1, after a first reading
Happy are those who read these words:
happy are those who hear them.

12.16 READING FROM THE BIBLE
From Revelation 1, after a Gospel reading
The word of God and the testimony of Jesus Christ. **Amen.**

12.17 READING FROM THE BIBLE
From Revelation 1–7, after a reading
Hear what the Spirit is saying to the churches. **Amen.**

OR

12.18 READING FROM THE BIBLE
From Revelation 1–7, after a reading
Hear what the Spirit is saying to the churches:
thanks be to God. Amen.

Hearing God's word to us

The Levites read from the Book of the Law of God, making it clear and giving the meaning so that the people could understand what was being read.

NEHEMIAH 8.7–8

Christ's message in all its richness must live in your hearts. Teach and instruct each other with all wisdom.

COLOSSIANS 3.16

13.1 HEARING GOD'S WORD TO US
Isaiah 55, before a sermon or address
Listen, listen to God; delight your soul in what is good:
Lord, we will listen that our souls may live. Amen.

13.2 HEARING GOD'S WORD TO US
From Matthew 17, before a sermon or address
We are in the presence of Jesus, the belovèd Son of God:
it is good to be here!

We have seen his glory:
let us listen to his voice. Amen.

13.3 HEARING GOD'S WORD TO US

From John 6, before a sermon or address

To whom shall we go but Jesus?

Lord, you have the words of eternal life.

13.4 HEARING GOD'S WORD TO US

From Hebrews 4

Lord, before your eyes everything is uncovered and laid bare: speak your word – living and active, sharper than any double-edged sword; let it penetrate our souls and spirits:

examine our thoughts,

and by your Holy Spirit renew

the attitudes of our hearts;

for Jesus' sake. Amen.

13.5 HEARING GOD'S WORD TO US

From James 1

Do not merely listen to the word, and so deceive yourselves; do what it says:

if we listen to God's perfect law,

it gives freedom;

and if we continue to do it,

and do not forget what we have heard,

we will be blessed in what we do.

Affirming our faith

In your hearts set apart Christ as Lord. Always be prepared to give an answer to everyone who asks you to give the reason for the hope that you have. But do this with gentleness and respect.

1 PETER 3.15

14.1 AFFIRMING OUR FAITH
From Psalm 89
Who is like the Lord?
There is no one like him –
he rules the raging sea,
he tames the mighty waves;
the heavens are his, the earth is his,
and all that live upon the earth are his.

Who is like the Lord?
There is no one like him –
his sceptre is righteousness,
his throne is justice,
his heralds are love and faithfulness.

Happy are those who come to praise the Lord:
they will walk in the light of his presence. Amen.

14.2 AFFIRMING OUR FAITH
From Psalm 126
We declare our faith in God:

Who brought us out from slavery?
The Lord! Thank you, Jesus.

Who filled our hearts with joy?
The Lord! Thank you, eternal Spirit.

Who has done great things for us?
The Lord! Thank you, Father.

Who gives us joy instead of tears; who gives us songs instead of
weeping; who blesses us with all good things?
The Lord our God:
Father, Son and Holy Spirit. Amen.

14.3 AFFIRMING OUR FAITH
From Psalm 145

We believe in God
who is gracious and compassionate,
slow to anger and rich in love.

We believe in God,
whose kingdom is everlasting,
whose dominion endures for ever.

We believe in God,
who is faithful to all his promises,
and loving towards all he has made.

We believe in God,
who opens his hand
and satisfies the needs
of all things living. Amen.

14.4 AFFIRMING OUR FAITH

From Isaiah 43

We believe in the Lord God,
the Holy One,
Father, Son and Holy Spirit;
we are his witnesses and his servants.
He alone is the Lord,
apart from him there is no saviour;
he has revealed and saved
and proclaimed;
he is our creator, our redeemer
and our king;
it is he who blots out our transgressions
and remembers our sins no more. Amen.

14.5 AFFIRMING OUR FAITH
From Isaiah 44
We believe in one God who made all things:

Did he stretch out the heavens, spread out the earth, and form us
in the womb?
He did!

Is he the Lord almighty, our king and redeemer?
He is!

Are we his own people, called by his name?
We are!

Does he pour his Spirit on us as on a dry and thirsty land?
He does!

We believe in one God, the Almighty,
Father, Son and Holy Spirit. Amen.

14.6 AFFIRMING OUR FAITH
From Isaiah 53, Passiontide
We believe in Jesus Christ,
the suffering Servant,
the Son of God;
he took upon himself our weaknesses
and carried our sorrows;
he was wounded for our sins
and beaten for our wickedness;
he was led as a lamb to the slaughter,
as a sheep before the shearers
he did not open his mouth;

he was put to death for our sins —
the sacrifice by which we are forgiven;
he bore the sin of many
and prayed for our forgiveness. Amen.

14.7 AFFIRMING OUR FAITH
From John 14, Pentecost, Trinity
We believe in God the Father
whom we have seen in Jesus Christ.

We believe in God the Son,
who is in the Father,
as the Father is in the Son.

We believe in God the Holy Spirit,
advocate with us for ever,
Spirit of truth whom the world cannot know:
we know him because he is with us and in us.

We believe in God almighty,
Father, Son and Holy Spirit. Amen.

14.8 AFFIRMING OUR FAITH

From Acts 2, Ascension, Pentecost, Trinity, Baptism

We believe in God the Father
who raised Jesus from the dead
and made him both Lord and Christ.

We believe in God the Son,
who was revealed to us with wonders and signs.
and nailed to a cross
at the hands of wicked men;
he was exalted to the right hand of the Father.
and received from the Father
the promised Holy Spirit.

We believe in the Holy Spirit
who was poured out upon us,
fruit of repentance and the forgiveness of sins,
promise and gift to us and our children
and to all near and far
whom the Lord our God will call.

We believe in one God,
Father, Son, and Holy Spirit. Amen.

14.9 AFFIRMING OUR FAITH
From Romans 1, Incarnation, Epiphany, Easter
We proclaim the Gospel, promised by God long ago through the
prophet, written for us in the Holy Scriptures:

**We believe in God the Father,
from whom grace and peace proceed,
whom we serve with our whole heart.**

**We believe in Jesus Christ;
as to his humanity,
born a descendant of David.**

**We believe in the Holy Spirit;
by whose power Jesus was declared to be the Son of God
through his resurrection from the dead.**

**We believe in Almighty God,
Father, Son and Holy Spirit. Amen.**

14.10 AFFIRMING OUR FAITH
From Romans 8, Pentecost
Christ's Spirit lives in you:
**our spirit is alive
because we have been put right with God.**

**The Spirit of God lives in you:
The Spirit is life for us –
even though our body dies,
God who raised Christ from the dead
will also give life to us
through his Spirit who lives in us. Amen.**

14.11 AFFIRMING OUR FAITH
From Romans 8, Ascension
We believe Christ Jesus died.
he was raised to life,
he is at the right hand of God,
he is interceding for us.

Who, then will condemn you?	**No one!**
Who shall separate us from the love of Christ?	**Nothing!**
Trouble?	**No!**
hardship?	**No!**
persecution?	**No!**
hunger?	**No!**
poverty?	**No!**
danger?	**No!**
death?	**No!**

We are certain that: nothing can separate us from the love of
Christ:
not death nor life,
not angels nor rulers nor powers,
not the present nor the future,
not height nor depth –
not the world above nor the world below –
nothing in all creation
will ever be able to separate us
from the love of God which is ours
through Christ Jesus our Lord. Amen.

14.12 AFFIRMING OUR FAITH
From 1 Corinthians 8 and 12
We believe in one God and Father;
from him all things come.

We believe in one Lord Jesus Christ;
through him we come to God.

We believe in one Holy Spirit;
in him we are baptized into one body.

We believe and trust in one God,
Father, Son and Holy Spirit. Amen.

14.13 AFFIRMING OUR FAITH
From Ephesians 3
Let us declare our faith in God:

We believe in God the Father,
from whom
       every family in heaven and on earth is named.

We believe in God the Son,
who lives in our hearts through faith,
and fills us with his love.

We believe in God the Holy Spirit,
who strengthens us with power from on high.

We believe in one God;
Father, Son and Holy Spirit. Amen.

14.14 AFFIRMING OUR FAITH
From Ephesians 3, Trinity
We are the family of God on earth and in heaven:

**Out of his glorious riches
God the Father strengthens us.**

**We receive inward power:
through the Holy Spirit.**

**Christ dwells within us
through faith.**

We believe in One God; Father, Son, and Holy Spirit.

In him we are rooted and established in love, and filled with the
measure of the fullness of God:
**to God be glory in the church
and in Christ Jesus
throughout all generations
for ever and ever. Amen.**

14.15 AFFIRMING OUR FAITH
From Ephesians 4
As God's people, let us declare our faith:

**There is one body and one Spirit,
just as we were called to one hope;
one Lord, one faith, one baptism:
one God and Father of all,
who is over all, and through all,
and in all. Amen.**

14.16 AFFIRMING OUR FAITH

From Philippians 2, Incarnation, Passiontide, Ascension

Let us affirm our faith in Jesus Christ the Son of God:

Though he was divine,
he did not cling to equality with God,
but made himself nothing.
Taking the form of a slave,
he became as we are;
as a man he humbled himself,
and was obedient to death –
even the death of the cross.
Therefore God has raised him on high,
and given him the name above every name:
that at the name of Jesus
every knee should bow,
and every voice proclaim
that Jesus Christ is Lord,
to the glory of God the Father. Amen.

14.17 AFFIRMING OUR FAITH
From Philippians 2 (Getting gradually quieter:)

Equal with God:
Jesus is Lord.

Emptied himself:
Jesus is Lord.

Came as a slave:
Jesus is Lord.

Found as a man:
Jesus is Lord.

Humbly obeyed:
Jesus is Lord.

Went to his death:
Jesus is Lord.

Death on a cross:
Jesus is Lord.

(Getting gradually louder:)

God raised him up:
Jesus is Lord.

Gave him the name:
Jesus is Lord.

Higher than all:
Jesus is Lord.

Every knee bow:
Jesus is Lord.

All tongues confess:
'Jesus is Lord!'

Glory to God! **Amen!**

14.18 AFFIRMING OUR FAITH

From Colossians 1

Let us confess our faith in the Son of God:

Christ is the image of the invisible God,
the firstborn over all creation.
By him all things were created:
things in heaven and on earth,
visible and invisible,
thrones, powers rulers, and authorities;
all things were created by him and for him.

He is before all things
and in him all things hold together.

He is the head of the body, the Church;
he is the beginning,
and the firstborn from the dead. Amen.

14.19 AFFIRMING OUR FAITH

From Colossians 1

God has rescued us
from the power of darkness,
and brought us safe
into the kingdom of his dear Son:
in Christ our sins are forgiven,
we are set free. Amen.

14.20 AFFIRMING OUR FAITH

From 1 Thessalonians 4 and 5, All Saints

Encourage one another with these words:
**We believe that Jesus died for us and rose again;
in order that we might live together with him,
whether we are alive or dead when he comes.**

We believe that God will take back with Jesus
those who have died believing in him.

**We believe the Lord himself will come
with a loud command,
with the voice of the archangel
with the trumpet call of God,**

We believe the dead in Christ will rise.

**We believe that we will be gathered up along with them
to meet the Lord.**

We believe we will always be with him.

So let us encourage one another and help one another. **Amen.**

14.21 AFFIRMING OUR FAITH
From 2 Thessalonians 2 and 3
Let us affirm the teaching to which we hold:

We believe in God the Father
who loved us,
and by his grace gave us
eternal encouragement and good hope.

We believe in God the Son
who assures our hearts
and strengthens us in every good deed
and word;
whose grace is with us all.

We believe in God the Holy Spirit,
the Lord of peace,
who gives us peace at all times
and in every way.

We believe in one God:
Father, Son and Holy Spirit. Amen.

14.22 AFFIRMING OUR FAITH
From 1 Timothy 2, Good Friday
There is one God and one mediator between God and us, Christ
Jesus, who gave himself as a ransom for all. **Amen.**

14.23 AFFIRMING OUR FAITH
From Titus 2 and 3

We believe the grace of God has dawned upon us with healing for all the world, and so we rejoice to declare our faith in him:

We trust in God the Father,
who has revealed his love
and kindness to us,
and in his mercy saved us,
not for any good deed of our own.
but because he is merciful.

We trust in Jesus Christ,
who gave himself up for us
to free us from our sin,
and set us apart for himself –
a people eager to do good.

We trust in the Holy Spirit,
whom God poured out on us generously
through Christ our saviour,
so that justified by grace
we might become heirs
with the hope of eternal life. Amen.

14.24 AFFIRMING OUR FAITH
From Titus 3
Let us declare our faith in God's salvation:

**We believe in God who saved us
not because of good things
we have done,
but because of his mercy.
God saved us
through the washing of rebirth
and renewal by the Holy Spirit,
who he poured out on us generously
through Jesus Christ our Saviour;
so that justified by his grace,
we might become heirs
with the hope of eternal life.**

This is a trustworthy saying. **Amen.**

14.25 AFFIRMING OUR FAITH
From Hebrews 1
**God who spoke to our ancestors
through the prophets
many times and in many ways,
in these last days has spoken to us by his Son,
whom he appointed heir of all things,
through whom he made the worlds:**

**The Son is the radiance of God's glory,
the likeness of God's being;
he sustains all things by his powerful word;
he achieved the forgiveness of sins
and sat down at the right hand
of the Majesty in heaven. Amen.**

14.26 AFFIRMING OUR FAITH
From 1 Peter 1
Let us proclaim our faith:

**We believe in God the Father,
by whose great mercy
we have been born again
to a living hope,
through the resurrection
of Jesus Christ from the dead.**

**We believe in God the Son,
who died for our sin,
and rose again for our justification.**

**We believe in God the Holy Spirit,
who bears witness with our spirit
that we are the children of God.**

**We believe in one God:
Father, Son and Holy Spirit. Amen.**

14.27 AFFIRMING OUR FAITH
From 1 Peter 3
Let us confess our faith in Christ:

**Christ died for sins
once for all,
the just for the unjust,
to bring us to God:
he was put to death in the body,
but made alive by the Spirit;
he has gone up on high,
and is at God's right hand,
ruling over angels and the powers of heaven.
Amen.**

14.28 AFFIRMING OUR FAITH
From 1 John 5
**We believe in God the Father,
who reveals his love to us in Christ.**

**We believe in God the Son,
who pours out God's Holy Spirit on us.**

**We believe in the Holy Spirit,
who teaches us God's truth.**

**We believe in one God:
Father, Son, and Holy Spirit. Amen.**

14.29 AFFIRMING OUR FAITH

From 1 John 5

We believe in Jesus Christ the Son of God,
and we have this truth in our hearts:
God has given us eternal life,
and this life is in his Son.

Whoever has the Son has life:
whoever does not have the Son of God
does not have life.

We believe that the Son of God has come:
he has given us wisdom
to know the true God. Amen.

14.30 AFFIRMING OUR FAITH

From Revelation 1, Easter

We believe in Jesus Christ, before whom we fall down and worship
but need not be afraid:
He is the first and the last,
the living one;
he has authority over death
and the world of the dead.

He was dead:
but now he is alive for ever and ever. Amen.

14.31 AFFIRMING OUR FAITH
From Revelation 1, Easter, Pentecost
Let us declare our faith in God:

We believe in God the Father;
the almighty,
who was, and is, and is to come.

We believe in Jesus Christ;
the faithful witness,
the firstborn from the dead,
the King of kings,
who loves us,
and has freed us from our sins by his blood.

We believe in the Spirit;
giver of many gifts,
proceeding from the throne on high.

We believe in one God:
Father, Son, and Holy Spirit. Amen.

14.32 AFFIRMING OUR FAITH

From Revelation 1, Advent

We believe in Jesus Christ:
he is the faithful witness,
he is the firstborn from the dead,
he is the ruler of the powers of the world.
He loves us –
he has loosed us from our sins by his blood.
He has made us a kingdom of priests
to serve our God.
He is coming on the clouds,
every eye will see him –
even those who pierced him.
All the peoples on earth will mourn
because of him.
So shall it be. Amen.

14.33 AFFIRMING OUR FAITH

From Revelation 1

We believe in Jesus Christ
before whom we fall down and worship
but need not be afraid:
he is the first and the last,
the living one;
he has authority over death
and the world of the dead,
for he was dead, but now is alive
for ever and ever. Amen.

14.34 AFFIRMING OUR FAITH
From Revelation 4, 5 and 22, All Saints

We believe in God the Father, who created all things:
**by his will they were created
and have their being.**

We believe in God the Son, who was slain; with his blood he
purchased us for God:
**from every tribe and language
and people and nation.**

We believe in God the Holy Spirit; the Spirit and the Bride say,
'Come!'
Even so, come, Lord Jesus! Amen.

15

Praying together

I urge that requests, prayers, intercession and thanksgiving be made for everyone – for kings and all those in authority, that we may live peaceful and quiet lives in all godliness and holiness; this is good, and pleases God our Saviour.

1 TIMOTHY 2.1–3
_____

Pray in the Spirit on all occasions with all kinds of prayers and requests. With this in mind, be alert and always keep on praying for all the saints.

EPHESIANS 6–18
_____

15.1 PRAYING TOGETHER
From Lamentations 3, before prayer
Let us open our hearts to God in heaven and pray:
Amen.

15.2 PRAYING TOGETHER
From Hebrews 4, Ephesians 3, etc., intercession
Let us approach God's throne with confidence.
we shall receive mercy,
and find grace to help
in time of need. Amen.

- For those in need …
  Upon … have mercy, Lord:
  we entrust them to your care.

- For the world …
  In … Lord, may peace and justice rule:
  let your love prevail.

- For the Church …
  O God, you are able to do immeasurably more than we ask or
  think by the power that is at work among us: …

  To Glory be to God in the Church and in Christ Jesus:
  for ever and ever. Amen.

15.3 PRAYING TOGETHER

From 1 Kings 8, after prayer
May the words we have prayed before the Lord our God be near
him day and night:
let all the people of the earth know
the Lord is God –
there is no other! Amen.

15.4 PRAYING TOGETHER
From Psalm 28, mercy

O Lord, our rock, we call to you:
do not refuse our cry.

O Lord, if you will not answer us, we are lost for ever:
Lord, hear our prayer
as we beg for your mercy;
as we call to you for help,
with hands uplifted in your presence.

O Lord, save your people; bless those who belong to you:
Lord, be our shepherd, and bless us always. Amen.

15.5 PRAYING TOGETHER
From Psalm 72, Harvest

Lord, judge your people in righteousness:
give justice to the oppressed.

Let the hills bring us prosperity:
the fruits of righteousness.

As long as the sun and the moon endure:
let rain fall upon the mown fields,
let showers water the earth.

Deliver the needy, who cry out for help:
the oppressed, who have no one to care for them.

Take pity on the poor and the helpless:
save them from death.

Rescue them from oppression and violence:
precious are their lives in your sight.

Bless the leaders of the people:
**let the people pray for them
and bless them every day.**

Let harvests ripen throughout the land:
let corn ripple across the hills.

Let orchards and forests flourish:
let fields and pastures be beautiful.

Praise to the Lord our God:
praise his glorious name for ever!

Let the earth be filled with his glory:
Amen and amen!

15.6 PRAYING TOGETHER

From Psalm 85, Rogation

O God, our Saviour,
you have been merciful to our land,
you have made us prosperous in the past,
you have forgiven us our sins
and pardoned our wrongdoing:
bring us back to faith,
make us strong again;
show us your constant love
and give us your saving grace,
help us to listen to what you are saying
and to leave our foolish ways,
so that we might receive your peace.

Lord, help us to honour you,
so that your healthful presence
may remain in our land:
then your love and our loyalty will meet,
our justice and your peace embrace;
our faith reach up from the earth
and your goodness look down from heaven;
you will bless us,
and our righteousness will prepare your way;
through Jesus Christ our Lord. **Amen.**

15.7 PRAYING TOGETHER
From Isaiah 33, grace
Lord,
be gracious to me,
for I long for you;
be my strength every morning,
and my help in time of trouble.
Thank you, Lord. Amen.

15.8 PRAYING TOGETHER
From Isaiah 35, holiness
Lord God,
lead us in the way of holiness,
cleanse us for our journey,
and teach us to be wise;
guard your redeemed,
crown your ransomed ones
with everlasting joy;
let sorrow and sighing flee away
and gladness overtake us;
in Jesus Christ our saviour. Amen.

15.9 PRAYING TOGETHER
From Isaiah 40, renewal
Lord, everlasting God, creator of the ends of the earth, you never grow tired or weary and no one can fathom your wisdom: when we feel weak increase in us your power, when we are tired refresh us, when we stumble and fall lift us up. Lord, you are our hope: renew us and strengthen us now and always. **Amen.**

15.10 PRAYING TOGETHER

From Isaiah 61, mission

Sovereign Lord, you have anointed us with your Spirit, and have sent us to preach good news to the poor, to bind up the broken-hearted, to announce freedom to the captives and release for the prisoners of darkness; to proclaim your grace and your judgement, to provide for those who mourn. Bless all to whom we go; bring your beauty into their lives – joy instead of mourning, praise instead of despair; through us, make them like trees you have planted – rooted in righteousness, that they may display your splendour; through Jesus Christ our saviour. **Amen.**

15.11 PRAYING TOGETHER
From Mark 13, Advent

When the skies grow dark and buildings fall, then hear us:
have mercy on us, Lord.

When deceivers come and the nations rise in anger, then hear us:
have mercy on us, Lord.

When the famines begin, and when the earth shakes to bring the future to birth, then hear us:
have mercy on us, Lord.

When we stand for a witness, when we are arrested and betrayed, then hear us:
have mercy on us, Lord.

When the sun is darkened and the moon fails to give us light, and the stars fall from the sky, then hear us:
have mercy on us, Lord.

When you come in your great power and glory with your angels from heaven, have mercy on us, Lord:
gather us from the four winds,
from the ends of the earth,
to be with you for ever. Amen.

15.12 PRAYING TOGETHER
From John 16
Jesus said, 'Ask and you will receive';
then our joy will be full. **Amen.**

OR

15.13 PRAYING TOGETHER
From John 16
'Ask and receive, and your joy will be full,'
Jesus spoke these words –
thanks be to God! Amen.

15.14 PRAYING TOGETHER
From Romans 8, Pentecost
Let the Spirit help you in your weakness when you do not know
what you ought to pray for:
the Spirit himself intercedes for us
with groans that words cannot express.

15.15 PRAYING TOGETHER
From 1 Thessalonians 4
We remember those who have fallen asleep in Christ:
with them we shall be with the Lord for ever.

We believe Jesus died and rose again:
so shall we live together with him.

God will take with Jesus those who have died believing in him:
let us encourage one another with these words. Amen.

16

Sharing Christ's peace

While the disciples were still talking about Jesus suffering and his rising from the dead, he stood among them and said to them, 'Peace be with you!'

LUKE 24.36

If you are offering your gift at the altar and there remember that your sister or brother has something against you, leave your gift there before the altar. First go and be reconciled with your brother; then come and offer your gift.

MATTHEW 5.23–26

16.1 SHARING CHRIST'S PEACE
From John 14
Peace to you all – not as the world gives:
our hearts will not be troubled.

Jesus' peace to you all:
we shall not be afraid. Amen.

16.2 SHARING CHRIST'S PEACE
From Romans 1

Grace and peace to you from God our Father and from the Lord Jesus Christ. **Amen.**

16.3 SHARING CHRIST'S PEACE
From Romans 15

The God of peace be with you all. **Amen.**

16.4 SHARING CHRIST'S PEACE
From 1 Corinthians 1

To the church of God in _____*, sanctified in Christ Jesus and called to be holy, to everyone who calls on the name of Jesus: grace and peace to you from God our Father and Jesus Christ our Lord. **Amen.**

16.5 SHARING CHRIST'S PEACE
From 2 Corinthians 13

The God of love and peace be with you. **Amen.**

16.6 SHARING CHRIST'S PEACE
From Galatians 6

Peace and mercy to the people of God. **Amen.**

16.7 SHARING CHRIST'S PEACE
From Ephesians 2, Unity

Peace to those who are near, and peace to those who come from away: **through Christ
we can all approach the Father
by one Holy Spirit. Amen.**

* Here supply the local name.

16.8 SHARING CHRIST'S PEACE

From Ephesians 6

Peace to our sisters and brothers, and love with faith from God the Father and the Lord Jesus Christ. **Amen.**

16.9 SHARING CHRIST'S PEACE

From Philippians 1

From God our Father and the Lord Jesus Christ, grace and peace to you all. **Amen.**

16.10 SHARING CHRIST'S PEACE

From 2 Thessalonians 1

Grace and peace to you from God our Father and the Lord Jesus Christ. **Amen.**

16.11 SHARING CHRIST'S PEACE

From 2 Timothy 1

Grace, mercy and peace from God our Father and Christ Jesus our Lord. **Amen.**

16.12 SHARING CHRIST'S PEACE

From Titus 1

Grace and peace from God our Father and Christ Jesus our Saviour. **Amen.**

16.13 SHARING CHRIST'S PEACE

From Philemon 1

Grace to you and peace from God our Father and the Lord Jesus Christ. **Amen.**

16.14 SHARING CHRIST'S PEACE

From 1 Peter 1

Grace and peace be yours in full measure. **Amen.**

16.15 SHARING CHRIST'S PEACE
From 1 Peter 5
Peace to all of you who are in Christ:
let us greet one another with love.

16.16 SHARING CHRIST'S PEACE
From 1 Peter 5 (variant)
Greet one another with love's embrace:
peace be to all who belong to Christ.

16.17 SHARING CHRIST'S PEACE
From 2 Peter 1
Grace and peace be yours abundantly through the knowledge of
God and of Jesus our Lord. **Amen.**

16.18 SHARING CHRIST'S PEACE
From 3 John
Peace to you all: greet your friends by name. **Amen.**
We greet one another

16.19 SHARING CHRIST'S PEACE
From Jude
God the Father has loved you and Jesus Christ has kept you safe:
mercy, peace and love be ours for ever. Amen.

16.20 SHARING CHRIST'S PEACE
From Revelation 1, Advent, Easter
Grace and peace to you from God who is, and who was, and who is
to come, and from Jesus Christ, the faithful witness, the firstborn
from the dead. **Amen.**

Offering our gifts to God

When you make a vow to God, do not delay in fulfilling it. It is better not to make a vow than to make a vow and not fulfil it. Do not let your mouth lead you into sin. And do not protest to the steward, 'My vow was a mistake.'

ECCLESIASTES 5.4–6

17.1 OFFERING OUR GIFTS TO GOD
From Genesis 33
Lord, you have been kind to us and have given us everything we need:
please accept the gifts
we bring to you today. Amen.

OR

17.2 OFFERING OUR GIFTS TO GOD
From Genesis 33
Lord, please accept these gifts that we have brought to you:
you have been kind to us,
and have given us everything we need. Amen.

17.3 OFFERING OUR GIFTS TO GOD

From Deuteronomy 15 and Matthew 10

Give to the Lord unselfishly and he will bless you in everything
you do:

Freely we have received –
let us freely give. Amen.

17.4 OFFERING OUR GIFTS TO GOD

From 1 Chronicles 29

Lord, we bring these gifts to honour your holy name:

they came from your hands
and they all belong to you. Amen.

17.5 OFFERING OUR GIFTS TO GOD

From Psalm 22

Among God's people, let us praise him for what he has done:

in the presence of those who worship him,
we offer God the sacrifices we have promised.
Amen.

17.6 OFFERING OUR GIFTS TO GOD

From Malachi 3 and Psalm 56

God says, 'Bring the full amount of your offering ... put me to the
test and you will see that I will open the windows of heaven and
pour out a blessing':

Lord, I will offer you what I have promised;
I will give you my offering of thanksgiving,
because you have rescued me from death
and kept me safe from defeat. Amen.

17.7 OFFERING OUR GIFTS TO GOD
From John 3 and Matthew 10

God so loved the world that he gave his only Son, so that all who
believe in him should not die but have eternal life:
Freely we have received –
let us freely give. Amen.

17.8 OFFERING OUR GIFTS TO GOD
From 2 Corinthians 8

Thank you, Lord Jesus Christ,
that, though you were rich,
yet for us you became poor
that we, through your poverty,
might become rich.
By your grace
let our riches supply the needs of others,
so that we may not have too much,
and they may not have too little;
for your name's sake. **Amen.**

17.9 OFFERING OUR GIFTS TO GOD
From Galatians 2 and Psalm 116

The Son of God loved us and gave his life for us: what can we offer
the Lord for all his goodness to us?
We will bring an offering to the Lord
to thank him for saving us;
in the assembly of all his people
we will give him what we have promised. Amen.

17.10 OFFERING OUR GIFTS TO GOD

From Philippians 4

Lord, you are all we have, and you give us all we need; our future is in your hands:
How wonderful your gifts to us;
how good they are!
To God our Father be glory for ever and ever.
Amen.

17.11 OFFERING OUR GIFTS TO GOD

From Philippians 4

To our God and Father,
who meets all our needs
according to his glorious riches in Christ Jesus,
be glory for ever and ever. Amen.

Inviting Jesus in/
Coming to Communion

(*see also* 'Drawing near to God')

Here I am! I stand at the door and knock. If anyone hears my voice and opens the door, I will come in and eat with him, and he with me.

REVELATION 3.20

18.1 INVITING JESUS IN
From Psalm 78
Lord, we have faith in you:
we trust your power to save.

You have spread for us a table in the wilderness:
rain down your blessing upon us;
give us the bread of angels,
satisfy us with your plenty. Amen.

18.2 INVITING JESUS IN

From Psalm 78 (variant)
Lord, we have faith in you:
we trust your power to save.

You have spread for us a table in the wilderness:
give us the bread of angels.

Pour down your mercy upon us:
satisfy us with your plenty. Amen.

18.3 COMING TO COMMUNION

From Luke 14
First minister
Blest are those who [*will*] eat
in the kingdom of God.
Second minister
Come, for all is now ready.

OR

18.4 COMING TO COMMUNION

From Luke 14
Blest are those who will eat
in the kingdom of God: come,
for all is now ready. **Amen.**

18.5 INVITING JESUS IN

From Luke 24, evening

It is evening, and the day is nearly over:

Lord, stay with us.

18.6 INVITING JESUS IN

From Revelation 3

Jesus says, 'Behold, I stand at the door and knock; if you hear my voice and open the door, I will come in and eat with you, and you may eat with me':

Lord, we hear your voice –
come in and eat with us.

Acclaiming the Saviour

Simon Peter answered, 'You are the Christ, the Son of the living God.'

MATTHEW 16.16

'Yes, Lord,' she told Jesus, 'I believe that you are the Christ, the Son of God, who was to come into the world.'

JOHN 11.27

19.1 ACCLAIMING THE SAVIOUR
From Isaiah 9
Jesus is the Wonderful Counsellor, The Mighty God, the Eternal Father, the Prince of Peace. **Amen.**

19.2 ACCLAIMING THE SAVIOUR
From Isaiah 11
We acclaim Jesus:
The Spirit of the Lord rests on Jesus – the Spirit of wisdom and of understanding, the Spirit of counsel and of power, the Spirit of knowledge and of the fear of the Lord. His belt is righteousness and faithfulness the sash round his waist. **Amen.**

19.3 ACCLAIMING THE SAVIOUR
From Isaiah 53

This is Jesus: he had no beauty in him that we should desire him; he was despised and rejected by men – a man of sorrows and acquainted with grief:

**he took up our weaknesses
and carried our sorrows;
he was pierced for our iniquities,
he was crushed for our sins;
the punishment that brought us peace fell on him
by his wounds we are healed.
Amen.**

19.4 ACCLAIMING THE SAVIOUR
From Matthew 17

We are in the presence of Jesus, the belovèd Son of God:
it is good to be here.

We have seen his glory:
let us listen to his voice. Amen.

19.5 ACCLAIMING THE SAVIOUR
From Luke 24

This is Jesus: behold his hands and his feet – believe he is risen from the dead! **Amen.**

19.6 ACCLAIMING THE SAVIOUR
From Colossians 1

Jesus is before all things, and in him all things hold together.
Amen.

19.7 ACCLAIMING THE SAVIOUR
From Colossians 1

Jesus is the image of the invisible God, the firstborn over all creation; by him all things in heaven and on earth were made; things, visible and invisible – thrones, powers, rulers, authorities; all things were created by him and for him. **Amen.**

19.8 ACCLAIMING THE SAVIOUR
From Hebrews 5

Jesus is God's Son; God is his Father; he is a priest after the order of Melchizedek:
he is able to deal gently with us when we go astray,
he is the source of our eternal salvation.
Hallelujah! Amen.

19.9 ACCLAIMING THE SAVIOUR
From John 1

We have found Jesus, the one of whom Moses and the prophets wrote:
Lord, we want to follow you. Amen.

19.10 ACCLAIMING THE SAVIOUR
From Revelation 1, Advent

Jesus is the Alpha and the Omega:
he is, he was, and he is to come. Amen.

19.11 ACCLAIMING THE SAVIOUR
From John 1, Christmas

Jesus is the Word of God; he became flesh and lived among us:
we have seen his glory,
the glory of the only Son of the Father,
full of grace and truth.

19.12 ACCLAIMING THE SAVIOUR
From Hebrews 1, Christmas, Christingle
This is Jesus: God's Son, appointed the heir of all things, through whom he made the universe, by whom God has spoken to us:
he is the radiance of God's glory
and the representation of God's being;
he sustains all things by his powerful word.

19.13 ACCLAIMING THE SAVIOUR
From Matthew 2, Epiphany
Jesus is born king of the Jews:
we have come to worship him.

19.14 ACCLAIMING THE SAVIOUR
From Matthew 3, Epiphany
This is God's Son, the belovèd:
with him God is well-pleased.

19.15 ACCLAIMING THE SAVIOUR
From John 1, Epiphany
We have found the Christ:
Jesus, you are the Son of God;
you are the king of Israel. Amen.

19.16 ACCLAIMING THE SAVIOUR
From John 1, Epiphany/Passiontide
Jesus is the Lamb of God:
he takes away the sins of the world.

19.17 ACCLAIMING THE SAVIOUR
From Mark 15, Passiontide
'He saved others – himself he cannot save':
truly, Jesus is the Son of God.

19.18 ACCLAIMING THE SAVIOUR

From Luke 24, Easter

This is Jesus: behold his hands and his feet – believe he is risen from the dead! **Amen.**

19.19 ACCLAIMING THE SAVIOUR

From Revelation 1, Easter

Jesus is the Living One:

he was dead –

behold, he is alive for evermore!

19.20 ACCLAIMING THE SAVIOUR

From Revelation 1, Easter

Jesus is the faithful witness, the firstborn from the dead, and the ruler of the kings of the earth:

to him who loves us

and has freed us from our sins by his blood,

be glory and power for ever and ever. Amen.

19.21 ACCLAIMING THE SAVIOUR

From Revelation 1, Easter, bereavement

Jesus is the Living One; he holds the keys of death and hell:

he was dead;

now he is alive for ever and ever!

Amen, hallelujah!

19.22 ACCLAIMING THE SAVIOUR

From Luke 24, Ascension

Jesus has been taken into heaven:

Lord, we worship you –

Hallelujah! Amen.

19.23 ACCLAIMING THE SAVIOUR
From Philippians 2, Ascension
God has exalted Jesus to the highest place and has given him the
name that is above every name:
at the name of Jesus let every knee bow,
in heaven and on earth and under the earth;
let every tongue confess
Jesus Christ as Lord,
to the glory of God the Father. Amen.

19.24 ACCLAIMING THE SAVIOUR
From Hebrews 1, Ascension
Jesus is God's Son, the sacrifice for sins. He is seated at the right
hand of the Majesty in heaven. Let all God's creatures worship him:
Lord, your throne will last for ever and ever,
righteousness will be the sceptre of your kingdom.

19.25 ACCLAIMING THE SAVIOUR
From Hebrews 9 and 10, Communion
Christ Jesus was sacrificed once to take away the sins of many:
we have been made holy
through the sacrifice
of the body of Jesus Christ
once for all.

Giving thanks to God

Give thanks to the Lord, for he is good; his love endures for ever.

PSALM 107.1

20.1 GIVING THANKS TO GOD
From Isaiah 59
We thank you, God our Father, that your arm is strong to save, and your ear ready to hear; we thank you that as you promised you have come to save your people who repent of their sins; we thank you that your Spirit is upon us and will not leave us, and we thank you that your word will not depart from us, nor from our children, nor from their children, from this time on for ever. **Amen.**

20.2 GIVING THANKS TO GOD
From Acts 4
We thank you, Sovereign Lord,
creator of sky, earth and sea
and everything in them,
that you spoke by your prophets:
stretch out your hand now to heal,
to perform miraculous signs
and wonders;
fill us with your Holy Spirit
that we too may speak boldly for you;
through the name of your holy servant, Jesus.
Amen.

20.3 GIVING THANKS TO GOD
From 1 Corinthians 12, Unity
We thank God for our unity in diversity:

There are different kinds of gifts:
but the same Spirit.

There are different kinds of service:
but the same Lord.

There are different kinds of working:
but the same God.

Praise to God almighty,
Father, Son and Holy Spirit,
who works in us
in all these ways. Amen.

20.4 GIVING THANKS TO GOD
From Ephesians 5
We give thanks for everything to God the Father:
in the name of our Lord Jesus Christ. Amen.

20.5 GIVING THANKS TO GOD
From Philippians 2, Ascension
We praise you, our God,
because you have exalted your Son Jesus Christ
to your right hand in glory,
and given him the name above every name,
that at the name of Jesus
every knee should bow.

Accept our worship, our love and thanksgiving;
and grant that we,
with those of every tongue,
may confess that Jesus Christ is Lord,
to your glory and honour. **Amen.**

20.6 GIVING THANKS TO GOD
From Revelation 2 and 3

Hear the promises of Jesus the first and the last, the living one, who was dead but now is alive for ever and ever, who has authority over death and the world of the dead:

Those who win the victory will eat from the tree of life:
thank you, Lord Jesus.

Those who win the victory will not be hurt by the second death:
thank you, Lord Jesus.

Those who win the victory will be given a new name:
thank you, Lord Jesus.

Those who win the victory will receive authority from the Father:
thank you, Lord Jesus.

Those who win the victory will be clothed in white, and their names will remain in the book of the living:
thank you, Lord Jesus. Amen.

Ministering God's grace

I remember your tears, and I want to see you very much, so that I may be filled with joy: keep alive the gift that God gave you when I laid my hands on you. The Spirit that God has given us does not make us timid; instead, his Spirit fills us with power, love, and self-control.

2 TIMOTHY 1.4–7

21.1 MINISTERING GOD'S GRACE
From Matthew 11
Come to Jesus with your weariness and your burden, and he will give you rest. **Amen.**

21.2 MINISTERING GOD'S GRACE
From John 6 and Isaiah 12
Jesus said, 'If you believe in me you will never be thirsty.'
**With joy I will draw water
from the wells of salvation. Amen.**

21.3 MINISTERING GOD'S GRACE
From Romans 8
God, who sees your heart hears the Spirit plead on your behalf and in accordance with his will:
***We* know that in all things God works for good
with those who love him. Amen.**

21.4 MINISTERING GOD'S GRACE

From Romans 8

You are God's *children* – possess the blessings he keeps for his people; possess with Christ what God has kept for him:
if *we* share Christ's suffering,
***we* will also share his glory. Amen.**

21.5 MINISTERING GOD'S GRACE

From 1 Thessalonians 5

Jesus died for us so that, whether we are awake or asleep, we may live together with him. **Amen.**

21.6 MINISTERING GOD'S GRACE

From 1 Timothy 1

Jesus came into the world to save sinners:
thanks be to God. Amen.

21.7 MINISTERING GOD'S GRACE

From 1 Timothy 2

God our Saviour wants all to be saved and to come to a knowledge of the truth. **Amen.**

21.8 MINISTERING GOD'S GRACE

From Titus 3

God our Saviour shows *you* his kindness and love not because of the righteous things *you* have done but because of his mercy. **Amen.**

21.9 MINISTERING GOD'S GRACE

From Hebrews 9

The blood of Christ, through the eternal Spirit, cleanse your conscience from acts that lead to death, so that you may serve the living God. **Amen.**

21.10 MINISTERING GOD'S GRACE
From 1 Peter 5
Cast all your burdens on to Jesus, for he cares for you.
Amen.

21.11 MINISTERING GOD'S GRACE
From John 3 and 1 John 4
God so loved the world that he gave his only Son, that all who
believe in him should not perish but gave eternal life:
This is love!
Not how we love God, but how he loved us –
he sent his only Son into the world
to be an atoning sacrifice for our sins,
that we might live through him –
Jesus Christ our Lord. Amen.

21.12 MINISTERING GOD'S GRACE
From Revelation 1
Jesus loves *you* and has saved *you* from your sins by his blood.
Amen.

21.13 MINISTERING GOD'S GRACE
From Revelation 1, bereavement
Look to Jesus and fall before him: he places his right hand on you
and says, 'Do not be afraid. I am the First and the Last. I was dead,
and behold, I am alive for ever.' **Amen.**

Giving God the glory

To you alone, O Lord, to you alone, and not to us, must glory be given because of your constant love and faithfulness.

PSALM 115.1

22.1 GIVING GOD THE GLORY
From Exodus 15, before song
Who is like you, O Lord, our God – majestic in holiness, awesome in glory, working wonders? In your unfailing love you will lead your redeemed;
in your strength you will guide us, Lord.

Let us sing to the Lord for he is highly exalted:
the Lord will reign for ever and ever. Amen.
♪

22.2 GIVING GOD THE GLORY
From Ephesians 3
Now to God the Father who is able to do immeasurably more than all we ask or think, by the power of the Spirit at work in us:
to him be the glory in the Church
and in Christ Jesus
throughout all generations
for ever and ever! Amen.

22.3 GIVING GOD THE GLORY
From Philippians 4
To our God and Father,
who meets all our needs
according to his glorious riches in Christ Jesus,
be glory for ever and ever. **Amen.**

22.4 GIVING GOD THE GLORY
From Jude
Now to him who is able to keep us from falling and to present us
before his glorious presence without fault and with great joy – to
the only God our Saviour be glory, majesty, power and authority,
through Jesus Christ our Lord, before all ages, now, and for evermore! **Amen.**

22.5 GIVING GOD THE GLORY
From 1 Timothy 6
To God the blest and only Ruler, the King of kings and Lord of
lords, who alone is immortal and who lives in unapproachable
light, whom no one has seen or can see; to him be honour and
might for ever. **Amen.**

22.6 GIVING GOD THE GLORY
From Revelation 4 and 5
You are worthy, O Lord our God:
to receive glory and honour and power.

For you created all things:
by your will they existed
and were created.

You are worthy, O Christ, for you were slain:
by your blood
you ransomed us for God.

From every tribe and tongue and people and nation, you made us a
kingdom and priests to serve our God:
Blessing and honour, glory and might
to him who sits upon the throne,
and to the Lamb;
for ever and ever! Amen.

Dedicating ourselves

Choose for yourselves this day whom you will serve ... but as for me and my household, we will serve the Lord.

JOSHUA 24.15

_____

23.1 DEDICATING OURSELVES
From Deuteronomy 26
Choose for yourselves this day whom you will serve:
We will serve the Lord!

You are witnesses against yourselves that you have chosen to serve the Lord:
Yes, we are witnesses.

Serve no other gods; yield your hearts to the Lord your God:
We will serve the Lord our God, and obey him. Amen.

23.2 DEDICATING OURSELVES
From Deuteronomy 26
**We declare this day
that the Lord is our God:
we will walk in his ways,
we will keep his decrees,
we will obey his commands
and live by his laws.**

The Lord declares this day that you are his own, his treasured possession; a people holy to the Lord your God, as he promised in Jesus Christ our Saviour:
Thanks be to God. Amen.

23.3 DEDICATING OURSELVES
From Psalm 101

Be careful to lead a blameless life:
this shall be our walk and our way.

Let the behaviour of your household be blameless:
we will not look upon evil.

Do not let the works of the ungodly contaminate you:
we will cleanse my heart from wickedness
we will have nothing to do with evil.

Meet with silence those who slander others:
we will not countenance the arrogant.

Take as your example those who are faithful and associate with them:
we will receive those whose character is blameless.

Do not welcome in those who practise deception:
no one who is a liar will find fellowship with us.

Every new day put to silence the wicked:
we will drive out all evil from the city of the Lord. Amen.

23.4 DEDICATING OURSELVES
From Psalm 119 (beginning verse 57)
Lord, you are my destiny:
I have vowed to heed your words.
With all my heart I seek your face:
be gracious to me as you have promised.

I have thought about my life:
I have turned around,
and I want to follow you.
I will not delay any longer:
I will obey you now.

Lord, the earth is full of your love:
teach me your commandments. Amen.

23.5 DEDICATING OURSELVES
From Mark 12
Our Lord God, you are the only Lord:
we will love you
with all our heart
and with all our soul,
with all our mind
and with all our strength;
and we will love our neighbours
as ourselves;

help us to obey your commandments:
and so to be ready
for the kingdom of God
in Jesus our redeemer. Amen.

23.6 DEDICATING OURSELVES

From Philippians 3
Lord,
whatever we once thought gain,
we offer you for the sake of Christ:
we long for him – to be found in him,
and, through faith in him
to gain the righteousness
that comes from you alone;
we want to know him,
the power of his resurrection
and the fellowship of his suffering;
to die to ourselves
that we might rise with him to eternal life. **Amen.**

23.7 DEDICATING OURSELVES

From 2 Chronicles 6, for a church building
O Lord our God, the only God whom the heavens cannot contain,
let alone this building which we *dedicate/consecrate* today, listen to
our cry as we come before you. Let your eyes be open towards this
place and hear the prayers of your people in this place:
hear from heaven, and forgive.

When we wrong our neighbours:
hear from heaven, and forgive.

When we have sinned against you, and when we turn back and
confess your name making supplication in this place:
hear from heaven and forgive.

When the skies are cloudless and there is no rain and your people
have sinned against you:
hear from heaven and forgive.

When famine or plague comes, or when there is disaster or disease
in the land:
hear from heaven and forgive,
teach us the right way to live.

When intercession is made by any of your people in trouble or
pain, and when they lift up their hands to pray in this place:
hear from heaven and forgive.

Lord, you know our heart –
make us to fear you and to walk in your ways
all the days of our life. Amen.

Lord God, let your eyes be open and your ears attentive to ...
this place:
let your ministers be clothed with salvation,
let your people rejoice in your goodness;
for the sake of your anointed One,
Jesus our Redeemer. Amen.

23.8 DEDICATING OURSELVES
From Song of Songs 8, Marriage
ᴹ Close your heart to every love but mine.
ᵂ Hold no one in your arms but me.

Pronouncing God's blessing

The Lord bless you and keep you; the Lord make his face to shine upon you and be gracious to you; the Lord turn his face towards you and give you peace.

NUMBERS 6.24–26

24.1 PRONOUNCING GOD'S BLESSING
From Joshua 22

(*Let us*) Love the Lord *your* God, walk in his ways, obey his commands, hold fast to him, serve him with all *your* heart and all *your* soul; and the blessing of God the Father, God the Son and God the Holy Spirit be upon *you* always. **Amen.**

24.2 PRONOUNCING GOD'S BLESSING
From 1 Kings 8

The Lord, the righteous God, make his face to shine upon *you*, the Lord fill *you* with a joy greater than all this world can give, the Lord make *you* to sleep in peace and to dwell in safety; and the blessing of God, Father, Son and Holy Spirit be with *you* now and always. **Amen.**

24.3 PRONOUNCING GOD'S BLESSING

From Job 29, commissioning

(*Let us*) Rescue the poor who cry for help, assist the orphans who have no one to save them, bless the dying, make the widow's heart sing; put on justice as *your* clothing, righteousness as *your* robe; be eyes to the blind and feet to the lame; care for the needy, champion the stranger in the name of Christ destroy the power of the evil one, and the blessing of God almighty, Father, Son and Holy Spirit be upon *you* wherever *you* go. **Amen.**

24.4 PRONOUNCING GOD'S BLESSING

From Psalm 3

The blessing of the Lord rest upon *you*:
salvation comes from the Lord. Amen.

24.5 PRONOUNCING GOD'S BLESSING

From Psalm 5

The Lord bless all who are righteous and love his name; the Lord in his favour shield and surround *you*; through Jesus Christ for ever. **Amen.**

24.6 PRONOUNCING GOD'S BLESSING

From Psalm 5

The Lord lead *you* in his righteousness, the Lord make his way clear before *you*, the Lord spread his protection over *you*, the Lord surround *you* with his love as with a shield; and the blessing of God almighty, the Father, the Son, and the Holy Spirit, be with *you* always. **Amen.**

24.7 PRONOUNCING GOD'S BLESSING
From Psalm 17

The Lord who loves *you*, fill *you* with his goodness, the Lord make *your* children to praise him, the Lord show *you* his face, the Lord bless *you* with a vision of himself when *you* awake; in the name of God, Father, Son and Holy Spirit. **Amen.**

24.8 PRONOUNCING GOD'S BLESSING
From Psalm 20

The Lord God answer *you* when *you* are in trouble, the Lord God be *your* protector, the Lord send *you* help from heaven and support from among his people, the Lord remember all *your* devotion and be pleased with *your* sacrifice of praise, the Lord give *you your* heart's desire and prosper *your* plans, the Lord grant *you* all *your* requests when *you* bow down and worship him:
Lord, answer us when we call to you. Amen.

24.9 PRONOUNCING GOD'S BLESSING
From Psalm 41

Blessing be upon you/*us who* care for the weak; the Lord deliver you/*us* in your/*our* time of trouble; the Lord protect and preserve you/*us*, the Lord bless you/*us* where you/*we* live, the Lord defend you/*us* from adversity, the Lord support you/*us* in sickness and in health; the Lord renew your/*our* life; in Jesus Christ for ever. **Amen.**

24.10 PRONOUNCING GOD'S BLESSING
From Psalm 56

(*Let us*) Walk in the presence of God in the light that shines on the living; and the blessing of God almighty, the Father, the Son and the Holy Spirit be among *you* and remain with *you* always. **Amen.**

24.11 PRONOUNCING GOD'S BLESSING

From Psalm 84

The Lord God almighty
be *your* sun and *your* shield:
The Lord withhold no good thing from *you*
as *you* walk before him in innocence.

The Lord almighty, Father, Son and Holy Spirit
bless *you* with happiness as *you* trust in him. **Amen.**

24.12 PRONOUNCING GOD'S BLESSING

From Psalm 115

(*Let us*) Receive the Lord's blessing:
the Lord will bless his people
and all the servants of God.

The Lord bless everyone who honours him, great and small alike;
the Lord, the maker of heaven and earth, bless *you*:
praise the Lord! Amen.

24.13 PRONOUNCING GOD'S BLESSING

From Psalm 119 (beginning verse 75)

The Lord's unfailing love comfort *you*, his servants, as he has
promised *you*, his goodness and mercy surround *you*, that *you* may
love his law and delight in it; in the name of our God, Father, Son,
and Holy Spirit. **Amen.**

24.14 PRONOUNCING GOD'S BLESSING
From Psalm 121

The Lord, the maker of heaven and earth, send *you* help from his holy place, the Lord who watches over his people and who never slumber nor sleeps watch over *you*; the Lord be at *your* right hand to shelter *you*, so that the sun will not hurt *you* by day, nor the moon by night; the Lord keep *you* from all harm, the Lord watch over *your* life (*lives*); the Lord watch over *your* coming and going both now and evermore. **Amen.**

24.15 PRONOUNCING GOD'S BLESSING
From Isaiah 11

The Spirit of the Lord rest upon *you*: the Spirit of wisdom and understanding, the Spirit of counsel and power, the Spirit of knowledge and the fear of the Lord; may *you* delight in the Lord, now and always. **Amen.**

24.16 PRONOUNCING GOD'S BLESSING
From Isaiah 40

The Lord *your* shepherd tenderly care for *you*, gather *you* in his arms, carry *you* close to his heart and gently lead *you*; and the blessing of God the Father, God the Son, and God the Holy Spirit, be with *you* always. **Amen.**

24.17 PRONOUNCING GOD'S BLESSING
From Isaiah 57

The Lord guide *you* and restore his comfort to *you*; the Lord bring praise to *your* lips; the Lord send *you* peace wherever *you* go; the Lord in his mercy heal *you*; and the blessing of God almighty, the Father, the Son and the Holy Spirit, be with *you* now and always. **Amen.**

24.18 PRONOUNCING GOD'S BLESSING
From Isaiah 57
The Lord look upon *your* need and heal *you*; the Lord guide *you*, the Lord restore comfort to *you*, the Lord give *you* his peace. **Amen.**

24.19 PRONOUNCING GOD'S BLESSING
From Isaiah 61
The Sovereign Lord anoint *you* with his blessing that *you* may preach good news to the poor, bind up the broken-hearted, proclaim freedom for the captives and release for those who are in darkness; that *you* may declare the Lord's favour and his judgement, and comfort those who mourn; so may the grace of our God, Father, Son and Holy Spirit, be upon *you* always. **Amen.**

24.20 PRONOUNCING GOD'S BLESSING
From Isaiah 65
The Lord make *you* glad and fill *you* with delight, the Lord grant *you* long life that *you* may enjoy the work of *your* hands, the Lord hear *you* before *you* call to him, the Lord answer *you* while *you* are still praying; the Lord bless *you* among his people and give *you* peace. **Amen.**

24.21 PRONOUNCING GOD'S BLESSING
From Luke 24, Ascension
Proclaim to all nations repentance for the forgiveness of sins, witness to the sufferings and rising of Jesus Christ, be clothed through the Holy Spirit with power from on high, worshipping with joy in the presence of God the Father; and the blessing of God the Father, God the Son and God the Holy Spirit be upon *you* all *your* days and wherever *you* go in Jesus' name. **Amen.**

24.22 PRONOUNCING GOD'S BLESSING

From Philippians 1

Live lives worthy of the gospel of Christ, stand together, defend the faith, do not be afraid; trust your Saviour, follow him, suffer for him: and the blessing of our God, Father, Son and Holy Spirit be upon *you* now and always. **Amen.**

24.23 PRONOUNCING GOD'S BLESSING

From Philippians 2

Be united in Christ, enjoy the comfort of his love, the fellowship of his Spirit, the tenderness and compassion of our God; and the blessing of God almighty, the Father, the Son and the Holy Spirit, be with *you* always. **Amen.**

24.24 PRONOUNCING GOD'S BLESSING

From Philippians 2

Shine like stars in a darkened world, hold out the word of life, be glad and rejoice in the Lord Jesus; and the blessing of God the Father, God the Son and God the Holy Spirit be with *you* always. **Amen.**

24.25 PRONOUNCING GOD'S BLESSING

From Philippians 2

(*Let us*) Continue to work out *your* salvation with fear and trembling, for it is God who works in *you* to will and to act according to his good purpose: and the blessing of God the almighty, Father, Son and Holy Spirit be upon *you* always. **Amen.**

24.26 PRONOUNCING GOD'S BLESSING
From Philippians 1 and 2

(*Let us*) Conduct *yourselves* in a manner worthy of the gospel of Christ. (*Let us*) Contend as one for the faith of the Gospel, being like-minded, having the same love, being one in spirit and purpose; and the blessing of God almighty, Father, Son and Holy Spirit be upon *you* always. **Amen.**

24.27 PRONOUNCING GOD'S BLESSING
From Philippians 3

(*Let us*) Forget what is behind, press on towards what is ahead, (*and*) reach out towards the goal to win the prize for which God has called *you* heavenwards in Christ Jesus: and the blessing of God almighty, Father, Son and Holy Spirit be upon *you* always. **Amen.**

24.28 PRONOUNCING GOD'S BLESSING
From Philippians 4

Rejoice in the Lord always, show gentleness to everyone; do not be anxious, make your needs known to God by prayer, with thanksgiving: and the peace of God guard *your* heart and mind in Christ Jesus. **Amen.**

24.29 PRONOUNCING GOD'S BLESSING
From Philippians 4

Whatever is true, whatever is honourable, whatever is just, whatever is pure, whatever is lovely, whatever is gracious; if there is anything excellent, or anything worthy of praise: (*let us*) think on these things: and the God of peace be with *you* always. **Amen.**

24.30 PRONOUNCING GOD'S BLESSING
From Philippians 4

May God meet all *your* needs from his glorious riches in Christ Jesus:

to God our Father be glory for ever and ever. Amen.

OR

24.31 PRONOUNCING GOD'S BLESSING
From Philippians 4

(*May*) God meet all *your* needs according to his glorious riches in Christ Jesus; and the blessing of Father, Son and Holy Spirit be with *you* daily for ever. **Amen.**

24.32 PRONOUNCING GOD'S BLESSING
From Colossians 3

Whatever *you* do, whether in word or deed, (*let us*) do it all in the name of the Lord Jesus, giving thanks to God the Father through him; and the blessing of God almighty, the Father, the Son and the Holy Spirit be upon *you* always. **Amen.**

24.33 PRONOUNCING GOD'S BLESSING
From Colossians 3, ministry, teaching

(*Let*) The word of Christ dwell in *you* richly as *you* teach and admonish one another with all wisdom; as *you* sing psalms, hymns and spiritual songs with gratitude in *your* heart(s) to God: and the blessing of God almighty, the Father, the Son and the Holy Spirit be upon *you* always. **Amen.**

24.34 PRONOUNCING GOD'S BLESSING

From Colossians 3, Easter, Ascension

Since *you* have been raised with Christ, (*let us*) set *your* hearts on things above, where Christ is seated at the right hand of God and the blessing of God almighty, the Father, the Son and the Holy Spirit be upon *you* always. **Amen.**

24.35 PRONOUNCING GOD'S BLESSING

From 1 Thessalonians 5, Easter, Ascension

Be joyful always: and the blessing of God the Father, God the Son and God the Holy Spirit be upon *you* now and evermore. **Amen.**

24.36 PRONOUNCING GOD'S BLESSING

From 2 Thessalonians 3, Easter, Ascension

The Lord direct *your* hearts into the love of God and the perseverance of Christ: and the blessing of God almighty, the Father, the Son and the Holy Spirit be upon *you* always. **Amen.**

24.37 PRONOUNCING GOD'S BLESSING

From 2 Timothy 1, for a minister/missionary

Fan into flame the gift of God, which is in you through the laying on of hands – the spirit of power, of love and of self-discipline; keep the pattern of sound teaching, with faith and love in Christ Jesus; with the help of the Holy Spirit who lives in us, guard the truth entrusted to you: and the blessing of God almighty, the Father, the Son and the Holy Spirit be upon *you* always. **Amen.**

24.38 PRONOUNCING GOD'S BLESSING

From Hebrews 10

Hold unswervingly to the hope you profess, for he who promised is faithful; consider how you may spur one another on towards love and good deeds – so encourage one another, and the blessing of God almighty, Father, Son and Holy Spirit be upon *you* now and until the Day of Christ. **Amen.**

24.39 PRONOUNCING GOD'S BLESSING

From Hebrews 12

Since *you* are surrounded by such a great cloud of witnesses, (*let us*) throw off everything that hinders and the sin that so easily entangles, and (*let us*) run with perseverance the race marked down for *you*; fix your eyes on Jesus, the author and perfector of *your* faith, who for the joy set before him endured the cross, scorning its shame, and sat down at the right hand of the throne of God. So may the blessing of God almighty, the Father, the Son and the Holy Spirit, be with *you* always. **Amen.**

24.40 PRONOUNCING GOD'S BLESSING

From Hebrews 12

Make every effort to live in peace with all and to be holy; without holiness, no one will see the Lord. And the blessing of God almighty, the Father, the Son, and the Holy Spirit be with you and remain with *you* always. **Amen.**

Dismissing the congregation

Jesus said to them, 'Go into all the world and preach the good news to all creation.'

MARK 16.15

25.1 DISMISSING THE CONGREGATION
From Exodus 33, evening
Lord God almighty, you have revealed your goodness to us and proclaimed your name among us:
now let your presence go with us,
and give us rest. Amen.

25.2 DISMISSING THE CONGREGATION
From Exodus 33, evening
The presence of the Lord go with you:
the Lord give us rest. Amen.

25.3 DISMISSING THE CONGREGATION
From 1 Kings 8, evening
Praise to the Lord, who has given rest to his people:
not one word of his promises has failed.

The Lord your God go with *you*:
may he never leave us or forsake us.

May he turn *your* hearts to him, to walk in his ways and to keep his commandments. **Amen.**

25.4 DISMISSING THE CONGREGATION
From Luke 24, Communion
The *Communion/Supper/Eucharist/Mass* is ended; Christ had to suffer and so to enter his glory: (*let us*) return at once and proclaim the good news to all, 'It is true, the Lord has risen!' and how *you* recognized Jesus in the breaking of bread. **Amen.**

25.5 DISMISSING THE CONGREGATION
From 1 Corinthians 16
Love to all of you in Christ Jesus:
the grace of the Lord Jesus be with us all.
Amen.

25.6 DISMISSING THE CONGREGATION
From Philippians 1
Rejoice and pray in the Spirit:
Jesus will set us free!

(*Let us*) Hope in God, believe; and (*let us*) have courage:
we are not ashamed!

Let Christ be exalted in *you*:
to live is Christ, to die is gain. Amen.

25.7 DISMISSING THE CONGREGATION
From 2 Timothy 2
Salvation is in Jesus Christ, and eternal glory:

If we die with him,
we shall live with him.

If we endure,
we shall reign with him. Amen.

25.8 DISMISSING THE CONGREGATION
From 2 Timothy 2
(*Let us*) Be strong through the grace that is in union with Christ
Jesus, take *your* part in suffering as his loyal soldier, remember him
who was raised from the dead, Jesus Christ, our Lord and Saviour.
Amen.

25.9 DISMISSING THE CONGREGATION
From Hebrews 13

Keep on loving each other as sisters and brothers, do not forget to entertain strangers, (*but*) remember those in prison as if *you* were their fellow prisoners, and those who are ill-treated as if *you yourselves* were suffering; (*let us*) honour marriage, keep *your* lives free from the love of money, (*and let us*) be content with what *you* have and the blessing of God almighty, Father, Son and Holy Spirit be upon you and remain with *you* always. **Amen.**

25.10 DISMISSING THE CONGREGATION
From Hebrews 13, Passiontide

Jesus suffered outside the city gates to make the people holy through his own blood. Let us go to him, bearing the distress he bore; for here we do not have an enduring city, but we are looking for a city that is to come; through Jesus, let us continually offer to God a sacrifice of praise – the fruit of lips that confess his name. (*Let us*) Go in peace. **Amen.**

25.11 DISMISSING THE CONGREGATION
From Revelation 22

Jesus says, 'Behold I am coming soon!' The Spirit and the bride say, 'Come!':
All who hear say, 'Come!'

Jesus, the faithful witness says, 'Yes, I am coming soon.'
Amen. Come, Lord Jesus.

The grace of the Lord Jesus be with all God's people. **Amen.**

Appendix: Services

The services which follow may be used freely subject to denominational rules of authorization. However, their dependence upon the Bible text offers the possibility of local ecumenical use where the need arises and denominational rules are satisfied.

Bible prayers for a Word Service

PREPARING FOR WORSHIP
From Psalm 19
May the words we say and sing and the thoughts of all our hearts be pleasing in your sight, O Lord, our Rock and our Redeemer. **Amen.**

GREETING ONE ANOTHER
From Romans 1
Grace and peace to you from God our Father and from the Lord Jesus Christ. **Amen.**

CALLING GOD'S PEOPLE TO WORSHIP
From Psalm 34
Glorify the Lord with me:
let us praise his name together.
Amen.

PROCLAIMING GOD'S PRAISE
From Psalm 98
Sing to the Lord, all the world:
the Lord is a mighty God.

Sing a new song to the Lord:
he has done marvellous things.

Proclaim his glory among the nations:
shout for joy to the Lord our king.
♪

DRAWING NEAR TO GOD –
Morning
From James 4 and Psalm 118
Draw near to God, and he will draw near to you. **Amen.**
Lord,
this is the day you made;
we rejoice and are glad in it:
help us and bless us
as we come into your presence –
we praise you and exalt you,
we celebrate and thank you;
for you are our God
and your love endures for ever.
Amen.

DRAWING NEAR TO GOD –

Evening
From James 4 and Psalm 134
Draw near to God, and he will draw
near to you. **Amen.**

Lord,
your servants come
in the evening of the day
to worship in your presence.
We lift up our hands to praise you
        in this holy place.
Lord, maker of heaven and earth,
we bless you now. **Amen.**

SEEKING GOD'S PARDON

From Isaiah 55
Seek the Lord while he may be
found; call on him while he is near;
forsake all wicked ways and all evil
thoughts.
Let us turn to the Lord,
that he may have mercy upon us,
and to our God,
who will freely grant us his pardon.

CONFESSING OUR SINS –

Morning
From 1 John 1
O God,
you have taught us
that if we say we have no sin
we deceive ourselves
and the truth is not us:
we humbly confess our sins to you;
and we ask you
        to keep your promise
to forgive us our sins
and to cleanse us
        from all unrighteousness;
through Jesus Christ our Lord.
Amen.

CONFESSING OUR SINS –

Evening
From Psalm 51
Lord God, be gracious to us
because of your great love for us;
for we are weighed down
        by our sins,
and know that we have failed;
we have offended against you
and done evil in your sight.
In your great mercy
        wash away our sins –
create in us a pure heart,
put a loyal spirit in us,
and give us again the joy
        that comes from your salvation.
Amen.

DECLARING GOD'S FORGIVENESS — *Morning*
From 1 John 4

Because God loves *you*, and by means of his Son whom he sent, *your* sins are forgiven. **Amen.**

DECLARING GOD'S FORGIVENESS — *Evening*
From Psalm 31

The Lord have mercy upon *you* in all *your* distress; the Lord deliver *you* from *your* sins and shelter *you* in all temptation; the Lord make his face to shine upon *you*, and save *you* in his unfailing love. **Amen.**

DECLARING GOD'S FORGIVENESS
From Psalm 103

God's love for those who seek him is as great as the heavens are high above the earth: as far as the east is from the west he removes your sins from you, and will remember them no more. **Amen.**

PROCLAIMING GOD'S PRAISE — *Morning*
From Psalm 95

Come, let us sing for joy to the Lord:
**let us shout
          to the Rock of our salvation.**

Let us come before him with thanksgiving:
and sing him joyful songs of praise! Amen.
♪

PROCLAIMING GOD'S PRAISE — *Evening*
From Revelation 19

Let us rejoice and be glad,
and give God the glory. Amen.
♪

READING FROM THE OLD TESTAMENT
From Jeremiah 9 and 2 Samuel 22
Before reading
Let us hear God's word:
let us listen to the Lord.

After reading
You are our lamp, O Lord;
you turn our darkness into light.

READING FROM THE NEW TESTAMENT

From Revelation 1

Before reading

The word of God and the testimony of Jesus Christ. **Amen.**

After reading

Happy are those who read these words:

happy are those who hear them.

READING FROM THE GOSPELS

From Mark 4

Those who have a mind to hear:

let them hear!

READING FROM THE EPISTLES & REVELATION

From Revelation 1

Hear what the Spirit is saying to the churches. **Amen.**

AFFIRMING OUR FAITH

From 1 Corinthians 8 and 12

We believe in one God and Father;

from him all things come.

We believe in one Lord Jesus Christ;

through him we come to God.

We believe in one Holy Spirit;

in him we are baptized into one body.

**We believe and trust in one God,
Father, Son and Holy Spirit. Amen.**

OR

AFFIRMING OUR FAITH

From Ephesians 3

Let us declare our faith in God:

**We believe in God the Father,
from whom every family
in heaven and on earth is named.**

**We believe in God the Son,
who lives in our hearts
    through faith,
and fills us with his love.**

**We believe in God the Holy Spirit,
who strengthens us with power
    from on high.**

**We believe in one God;
Father, Son and Holy Spirit.
Amen.**

THE LORD'S PRAYER

From Matthew 6 and Luke 11

**Our Father in heaven,
hallowed be your name,
your kingdom come,
your will be done,
on earth as in heaven.**

Give us today our daily bread.
Forgive us our sins
as we forgive those
who sin against us.
Lead us not into temptation
but deliver us from evil.

For the kingdom, the power,
and the glory are yours,
now and for ever. Amen.

PRAYING TOGETHER
From Lamentations 3
Let us open our hearts to God in
heaven and pray. **Amen.**

• **For those in need**
From Psalm 31
Be merciful, Lord, to all who are in
trouble:
Lord, we entrust them to your care.

All who are tired and all who are weak:
Lord, we entrust them to your care.

All who are deep in sorrow and all
whose life is ebbing away:
Lord, we entrust them to your care.

All who are without friends and all
who are forgotten by the world:
Lord, we entrust them to your care;
in Jesus' name. Amen.

• **For the world**
From Psalm 82
Come, Lord God, and rule the world:
all the nations are yours.

Let laws be just, let justice be impar-
tial, let the rights of the poor and of
children be defended:
come, Lord God, and rule the world.

Help us to rescue the innocent from
the power of evil:
come, Lord God, and rule the world.

Let the ignorant be taught, let cor-
ruption be purged, let righteousness
prevail:
come, Lord God, and rule the world.

Come, Lord God, and rule the world:
all the nations are yours. Amen.

• **For ourselves**
From 2 Thessalonians 2
God our Father,
in your love you have given us
eternal hope:
encourage our hearts,
and strengthen us
in every good deed and word;
let the Spirit of peace
bring us peace always
and in every way;

and the grace of our Lord Jesus Christ
be with us all. **Amen.**

GIVING THANKS TO GOD

From Psalm 107

Let us give thanks to the Lord for his
unfailing love. **Amen.**

SAYING 'THE GRACE'

From 2 Corinthians 13

The grace of our Lord Jesus Christ,
and the love of God,
and the fellowship of the Holy Spirit,
be with us all evermore. **Amen.**

HEARING GOD'S WORD TO US

From Jeremiah 9

Let us listen to the Lord. **Amen.**

OR

HEARING GOD'S WORD TO US

From Hebrews 4

Lord, before your eyes everything is
uncovered and laid bare: speak your
word, living and active, sharper than
any two-edged sword; let it penetrate
our souls and spirits:
examine our thoughts,
and by your Holy Spirit renew
our hearts and lives;
for Jesus' sake. Amen.

OFFERING GOD OUR GIFTS

From Philippians 4

To our God and Father, who meets
all our needs according to his glorious riches in Christ Jesus:
be glory for ever and ever. Amen.

GIVING GOD THE GLORY

From 1 Timothy 1

Now to the king eternal, immortal,
invisible, the only God:
be honour and glory
for ever and ever. Amen.

OR

GIVING GOD THE GLORY

From Jude

Now to him who is able to keep us
from falling and to present us fault-
less before his glorious presence with
great joy – to the only God our Saviour be glory, majesty, power and
authority, through Jesus Christ our
Lord, before all ages, now, and for
evermore! **Amen.**

PRONOUNCING GOD'S BLESSING

From Numbers 6

The Lord bless *you* and keep *you*, the Lord make his face to shine upon *you*, the Lord be kind and gracious to *you*, the Lord look upon *you* with favour, and give *you* peace. **Amen.**

DISMISSING THE CONGREGATION

From Isaiah 55

Let us go out with joy:
let us depart in peace. Amen.

DISMISSING THE CONGREGATION – *Evening*

From Exodus 33

The presence of the Lord go with *you*: **the Lord give us rest. Amen.**

Bible prayers for a
Short 'Office' Service

PREPARING FOR WORSHIP

From Psalm 19

Let us pray:

**May the words we say or sing
and the thoughts of all our hearts
be pleasing in your sight, O Lord,
our Rock and our Redeemer. Amen.**

CONFESSING OUR SINS

From 1 John 1

**O God,
you have taught us
that if we say we have no sin
we deceive ourselves
and the truth is not in us:
humbly we confess our sins to you
and ask you to keep your promise
to forgive us our sins
and to cleanse us
from all unrighteousness;
through Jesus Christ our Lord.
Amen.**

**DECLARING GOD'S
FORGIVENESS**

From 1 John 4

Because God loves you/*us*, and by
means of his Son whom he sent,
your/*our* sins are forgiven. **Amen.**

SAYING OR SINGING A PSALM

See Psalm section.

READING FROM THE BIBLE

From Jeremiah 9 and 1 Peter 1

Before a reading:

Let us hear God's word:

let us listen to the Lord.

After a reading:

The word of the Lord remains for ever.
Amen.

AFFIRMING OUR FAITH

From 1 Corinthians 8 and 12

We believe in one God and Father;
from him all things come.

We believe in one Lord Jesus Christ;
through him we come to God.

We believe in one Holy Spirit;
**in him we are baptized
    into one body.**

**We believe and trust in one God,
Father, Son and Holy Spirit. Amen.**

THE LORD'S PRAYER

From Matthew 6 and Luke 11

**Our Father in heaven,
hallowed be your name,
your kingdom come,
your will be done,
on earth as in heaven.
Give us today our daily bread.
Forgive us our sins
as we forgive those
    who sin against us.
Lead us not into temptation
but deliver us from evil.**

**For the kingdom, the power,
    and the glory are yours,
now and for ever. Amen.**

PRAYING TOGETHER

*From Lamentations 3 and
Philippians 4*

Before intercessions

Let us open our hearts to God in
heaven and pray. **Amen.**

After intercessions

To our God and Father, who meets
all our needs according to his glorious riches in Christ Jesus:
be glory for ever and ever. Amen.

SAYING 'THE GRACE'

From 2 Corinthians 13

The grace of our Lord Jesus Christ,
and the love of God,
and the fellowship of the Holy Spirit,
be with us all evermore. **Amen.**

PRONOUNCING GOD'S BLESSING

From Psalm 129

The blessing of the Lord be upon you:
**we bless you
in the name of the Lord. Amen.**

DISMISSING THE CONGREGATION

From Isaiah 55

Let us go out with joy:
let us depart in peace. Amen.

Psalms

PSALM 34A

I will bless the Lord at all times:
his praise will be always on my lips.

I will glory in the Lord:
let those who are sad
hear and rejoice.

Glorify the Lord with me:
let us praise him together!

I asked the Lord to help me, and he
answered me:
he set me free from my fear.

Those who turn to him are radiant:
shame will not cover their faces.

Whenever someone in need prays,
the Lord hears and will come to the
rescue:
The angel of the Lord
will guard those who obey him
and will save.

Taste and see how good is the Lord:
happy are those who come to him.

Obey the Lord, you people of the
Lord:
those who obey him lack nothing.

PSALM 36

Your love, O Lord reaches the heavens:
your faithfulness extends to the
skies.

Your righteousness is like the towering mountains:
your justice is like the great deep.

How precious is your love, O God:
we find shelter under your wings!

We feast on the food you provide:
we drink from the river
of your goodness.

For with you is the fountain of life:
in your light we see light. Amen.

PSALM 100

Rejoice in the Lord, all the earth:
worship the Lord with gladness.

Remember the Lord is our God:
we are his flock and he made us.

Come to his temple with praise:
enter his gates with thanksgiving.

The love of the Lord will not fail:
God will be faithful for ever. Amen.

Bible prayers for a Communion Service

GREETING ONE ANOTHER
From Ruth 2
The Lord be with you:
the Lord bless you!

PROCLAIMING GOD'S PRAISE
From Psalm 96
Sing to the Lord a new song:
proclaim his salvation each day.

Declare his glory to all:
he is great and is worthy of praise.
Amen.
♪

CALLING GOD'S PEOPLE TO WORSHIP
From James 4
Come near to God, and he will come near to you; wash your hands and purify your heart:
let us humble ourselves
before the Lord,
that he may lift us up.

DRAWING NEAR TO GOD
From Psalm 26
Lord God,
we are here to worship you –
let your love guide us,
and your faithfulness lead us;
we come to ask for your forgiveness,
to gather round your table,
to proclaim your redemption
and to bring you our thanksgiving:
receive the praise of your people.
Amen.

OR

PREPARING FOR WORSHIP
From Psalm 51
God of unfailing love and mercy,
wash away our wickedness
and cleanse us from our sin;
create in us a pure heart,
and strengthen our spirits within us;
renew in us the joy of your salvation
– open our lips,
and we will praise you. Amen.

HEARING JESUS' COMMANDMENTS

From Mark 12

Jesus said: Love the Lord your God with all your heart and with all your soul and with all your mind and with all your strength; and love your neighbour as yourself.

CONFESSING OUR SINS

From Amos 2

Lord God almighty,
we have rejected your law,
and have not obeyed
        your commandments;
we have sinned,
and dishonoured your holy name:
have mercy on us;
for Jesus' sake. Amen.

DECLARING GOD'S FORGIVENESS

From Psalm 6

The Lord God be merciful to *you* and heal *you*; the Lord turn his face towards *you* and deliver *you*; the Lord save *you* in his unfailing love; through Jesus Christ. **Amen.**

OR

DECLARING GOD'S FORGIVENESS

From Psalm 103

God who is merciful and loving will not punish *you* as *you* deserve, nor repay *you* for *your* sins and wrongdoing. As high as the sky is above the earth, so great is his love for *you*; as far as the east is from the west, so far has he removed *your* sins from *you*; through Jesus Christ our Lord. **Amen.**

RECEIVING GOD'S MERCY

From Isaiah 12

Surely God is our salvation; we will trust and not be afraid:
The Lord, the Lord,
is my strength and my song –
he has become my salvation. Amen.

PRAYING TOGETHER

From Hebrews 4, Ephesians 3, etc.

Let us approach God's throne with confidence:
we shall receive mercy,
and find grace to help
        in time of need.

• **For those in need**
Upon ... have mercy, Lord:
we entrust them to your care.

• **For the world**

In ... Lord, let peace and justice rule:
let your love prevail.

• **For the Church**

O God, you are able to do immeasurably more than all we ask or think by the power that is at work among us ...

To God be glory in the Church and in Christ Jesus:
for ever and ever. Amen.

SAYING A PSALM TOGETHER

From Psalm 36

Your love, O Lord, reaches the heavens:
your faithfulness extends to the skies.

Your righteousness is like the towering mountains:
your justice is like the great deep.

How precious is your love, O Lord:
we find shelter under your wings!

We feast on the food you provide:
we drink from the river of your goodness.

For with you is the fountain of life:
in your light we see light. Amen.

READING FROM THE BIBLE

From 1 Peter 1

The word of the Lord remains for ever.
Amen.

READING FROM THE GOSPELS

From 1 Peter 1

This is the Gospel we proclaim.
Amen.

AFFIRMING OUR FAITH

From Titus 2 and 3

The grace of God has dawned upon us with healing for all the world; in this we trust, and say:

**We believe in God the Father,
who revealed his love
and kindness to us,
and in his mercy saved us,
not for any good deed of our own.
but because he is merciful.**

**We believe in Jesus Christ,
who gave himself up for us
to free us from our sin,
and set us apart for himself –
a people eager to do good.**

We believe in the Holy Spirit,
whom God poured out on us
    generously
through Christ our saviour,
so that justified by grace
we might become heirs
with the hope of eternal life. Amen.

HEARING GOD'S WORD TO US
*From Jeremiah 9, before sermon or
address*
Let us hear God's word:
let us listen to the Lord.

OR

HEARING GOD'S WORD TO US
*From Psalm 130, before sermon or
address*
We wait eagerly for the Lord:
in his word we trust. Amen.

DRAWING NEAR TO GOD
From Hebrews 10
Have confidence to enter the most
holy place by the blood of Jesus:
**let us draw near to God
with a sincere heart
in full assurance of faith. Amen.**

SHARING CHRIST'S PEACE
From 2 Corinthians 13
The God of love and peace be with
you. **Amen.**

From Romans 15
Welcome one another as Christ has
welcomed you:
to God be the glory. Amen.

OR

From 1 Peter 5
Peace to you all in Christ: greet one
another in love. [**Amen.**]
(We greet each other)

COMING TO COMMUNION
From Luke 14
Blest are those who eat in the kingdom of God: come, for all is now
ready. **Amen.**

OFFERING GOD OUR GIFTS
1 Chronicles 29
Lord, we bring these gifts to honour
your holy name:
**they came from your hands
and they all belong to you. Amen.**

GIVING THANKS TO GOD
From 2 Timothy 4, Lamentations 3 and Psalm 23

The Lord be with your spirit:
grace be with you.

Let us lift our hearts and our hands to God in heaven and pray. **Amen.**

WELCOMING JESUS IN
From Matthew 17

We are in the presence of Jesus:
Lord, it is good to be here!

ACCLAIMING THE SAVIOUR
From John 1

Behold the Lamb of God:
**Jesus takes away
the sins of the world.**

GIVING THANKS TO GOD
From Ruth 2 and Psalm 107

The Lord be with you:
the Lord bless you.

Let us give thanks to the Lord:
his mercy lasts for ever.

He satisfies the thirsty:
**and fills the hungry
with good things.**

From Psalm 78

Lord, we have faith in you:
we trust your power to save.

You have spread for us a table in the wilderness:
give us the bread of angels.

Rain down your blessing upon us:
satisfy us with your plenty. Amen.

From Ephesians 5, Psalms 23 and 36

In the name of our Lord Jesus Christ we give thanks for everything to God the Father.

Lord, in the sight of the world:
you have set a feast before us.

You anoint us as your guests:
you fill our cup with joy.

We thank you, our Father, that your love reaches to the heavens, and your faithfulness to the skies; that your justice is deep like the seas. Your unfailing mercies cannot be bought, yet we feast on your goodness and drink from the river of your blessing. [Especially we thank you *that/for* ...]

From Isaiah 6
God, our Father, high and exalted, but present among us, with angels and saints in heaven we cry to each other:
Holy, holy, holy,
the Lord almighty is holy,
his glory fills the world.

From 1 Corinthians 10 and 11
And now we thank you that our Lord Jesus Christ in the night he was betrayed, took bread, and when he had given thanks, he broke it and said, 'This is my body, given for you; do this to remember me':
we break this bread
to share in the body of Christ.

In the same way, after supper, he took the cup, saying, 'This cup is the new covenant in my blood; do this, whenever you drink it, to remember me':
we drink this cup
to share in the blood of Christ.

From Colossians 1, Hebrews 13 and Psalm 50
Eternal Father, in your presence we declare the mystery of your love for us and honour you with our sacrifice of praise and thanksgiving. So we prepare your way before you:
show us your salvation.

From Romans 5 and John 6
Pour out your love into our hearts by the Holy Spirit whom you have given to us, and let this bread and wine be for us the body and blood of Christ, food of our eternal life. **Amen.**

From Revelation 5
Worthy is the Lamb who was slain,
to receive power and wealth,
wisdom and strength,
honour and glory and praise. Amen.

From 1 Corinthians 12 and Revelation 22
Whenever you eat this bread and drink this cup you proclaim the Lord's death until he comes:
Amen. Come, Lord Jesus.

HEARING GOD'S INVITATION
From James 4
Draw near to God, and he will draw near to you. **Amen.**

THE LORD'S PRAYER
From Matthew 6 and Luke 11
The Lord has taught us to pray:
Our Father in heaven,
hallowed be your name,
your kingdom come,
your will be done,
on earth as in heaven.

Give us today our daily bread.
Forgive us our sins
as we forgive those
        who sin against us.
Lead us not into temptation
but deliver us from evil.

For the kingdom, the power,
        and the glory are yours,
now and for ever. Amen.

RECEIVING THE BREAD AND
THE WINE
From John 6
Come to Jesus, and you will never go
hungry. **Amen.**

Believe in Jesus, and you will never
be thirsty. **Amen.**

MINISTERING GOD'S GRACE
From Revelation 1
Jesus loves you, and has saved you
from your sins by his blood. **Amen.**

OR

MINISTERING GOD'S GRACE
From 1 Peter 5
Cast all your burdens on to Jesus, for
he cares for you. **Amen.**

GIVING GOD THE GLORY
From Psalm 63, after Communion
Lord God, our God, we have seen you
in the sanctuary:
**we have looked on your power
and your glory.**

Because your love is better than life
our lips will glorify you:
we will praise you as long as we live.

In your name we will lift up our
hearts:
Glory be to you, Lord God. Amen.
♪

OR

GIVING GOD THE GLORY
From Romans 16, after Communion
The grace of our Lord Jesus Christ be
with you:
**Glory to God,
who alone is all-wise;
through Jesus Christ, for ever!
Amen.**

PRONOUNCING GOD'S
BLESSING
From Psalm 129
The blessing of the Lord be upon you:
**we bless you
in the name of the Lord. Amen.**

**DISMISSING THE
CONGREGATION**
From Isaiah 55
Let us go out with joy:
let us depart in peace. Amen.

OR

**DISMISSING THE
CONGREGATION**
From Exodus 33, evening
The presence of the Lord go with *you*:
the Lord give us rest. Amen.

Bible prayers for a
Short Communion Service

PROCLAIMING GOD'S PRAISE

From Psalm 96

Sing to the Lord a new song:
proclaim his salvation each day.

Declare his glory to all:
he is great and worthy of praise.
Amen.

GREETING ONE ANOTHER

From Ruth 2

The Lord be with you:
the Lord bless you.

DRAWING NEAR TO GOD

From Psalm 26

Lord God,
we are here to worship you –
let your love guide us,
and your faithfulness lead us;
we come to ask for your forgiveness,
to gather round your table,
to bring you our thanksgiving,
and to proclaim your redemption:
receive the praise of your people.
Amen.

HEARING GOD'S
COMMANDMENTS

From Mark 12

Jesus said: Love the Lord your God
with all your heart and with all your
soul and with all your mind and with
all your strength; and love your
neighbour as yourself.
Lord, we have broken
        your commandments:
forgive us, and help us to obey.
Amen.

CONFESSING OUR SINS

From 1 John 1

God our Father,
you have taught us
that if we say we have no sin
we deceive ourselves
and the truth is not in us:
we humbly confess our sins to you,
and we ask you to keep your promise
to forgive us our sins
and to cleanse us
        from all unrighteousness;
through Jesus Christ our Lord. Amen.

DECLARING GOD'S FORGIVENESS
From Psalm 6

The Lord God be merciful to *you* and heal *you*; the Lord turn his face towards *you* and deliver *you*; the Lord save *you* in his unfailing love; through Jesus Christ. **Amen.**

CALLING GOD'S PEOPLE TO WORSHIP
From Psalm 107

Let us give thanks to the Lord:
his mercy lasts for ever.

He satisfies the thirsty:
and fills the hungry
with good things. Amen.

READING FROM THE BIBLE
Before Reading
From Jeremiah 9

Let us listen to the Lord,
let us pay attention to his word.

After Reading
From Revelation 1

Hear what the Spirit is saying to the churches:
thanks be to God. Amen.

AFFIRMING OUR FAITH
From Titus 2 and 3

Let us confess our faith in one God, whose grace has dawned upon the world.

We believe in God the Father,
who has revealed
his loving kindness to us,
and in his mercy saved us –
not for any good deed of our own,
but because he is merciful.

We believe in God the Son,
who sacrificed himself for us
to free us from our sin,
and make us his own people,
holy, and eager to do good.

We believe in one Holy Spirit,
whom God poured out on us
generously
through Christ our saviour;
so that justified by his grace
we might become heirs
to eternal life. Amen.

PRAYING TOGETHER
From Hebrews 4
Let us approach God's throne with confidence:
we shall receive mercy,
and find grace to help
in time of need. Amen.

Upon ... have mercy, Lord;
we entrust them to your care.

In ... Lord, may peace and justice rule:
let your love prevail.

To God be glory in the Church and in Christ Jesus:
for ever and ever. Amen.

SHARING CHRIST'S PEACE
From 1 Peter 5
Peace to you all in Christ: greet one another in love. **Amen.**

OFFERING OUR GIFTS
From 1 Chronicles 29
Yours, Lord is the greatness,
the power and the glory,
the splendour and the majesty;
everything comes from you,
and of your own do we give you.
Amen.

GREETING ONE ANOTHER
From 2 Timothy 4
The Lord be with your spirit:
grace and peace be with you.

GIVING THANKS TO GOD
From Ephesians 5, Isaiah 6, Romans 5,
John 6, 1 Corinthians 11, and Psalm 19
In the name of our Lord Jesus Christ we give thanks for everything to God the Father. Father, we thank you for all your goodness, especially for ...

Lord, high and exalted, yet present among us, with angels and saints in heaven we call to each other:
Holy, holy, holy,
the Lord almighty is holy,
his glory fills the world. Amen.

Pour out your love into our hearts by the Holy Spirit whom you have given to your people. Let this bread and wine be to us the body and blood of Christ, food of our eternal life.

For our Lord Jesus Christ
in the night he was betrayed,
took bread,
and when he had given thanks,
he broke it and said,
'This is my body, which is for you;
do this to remember me.'

In the same way, after supper,
he took the cup, saying,
'This cup is the new covenant
in my blood;
do this, whenever you drink it,
to remember me.'

So may our remembrance
be acceptable in your sight,
O Lord our strength and our
redeemer. **Amen.**

THE LORD'S PRAYER
From Matthew 6 and Luke 11
Our Father in heaven,
hallowed be your name,
your kingdom come,
your will be done,
on earth as in heaven.
Give us today our daily bread.
Forgive us our sins
as we forgive those
    who sin against us.
Lead us not into temptation
but deliver us from evil.

For the kingdom, the power,
    and the glory are yours,
now and for ever. Amen.

MINISTERING GOD'S GRACE
From John 6
Jesus said, 'If you come to me you
will never go hungry.' **Amen.**

Jesus said, 'If you believe in me you
will never be thirsty.' **Amen.**

GIVING GOD THE GLORY
From Romans 16
Glory to God
who alone is all-wise;
through Jesus Christ, for ever! **Amen.**

PRONOUNCING GOD'S BLESSING
From 2 Thessalonians 3
The Lord of peace give *you* peace
at all times and in every way;
and the blessing of God almighty,
the Father, the Son
    and the Holy Spirit,
be with *you* always. **Amen.**

DISMISSING THE CONGREGATION
From John 20, morning
Jesus said, 'As the Father has sent me,
so I am sending you.' Go in the name
of Christ. **Amen.**

DISMISSING THE CONGREGATION
From Exodus 33, evening
The presence of the Lord go with you:
the Lord give us rest. Amen.

Bible Reference Index

2. Salvation is in Jesus Christ – 25.7
4.22 The Lord be with your spirit – 3.19ar

TITUS

1.4 Grace and peace from God our Father – 3.20
1.4 Grace and peace from God our Father – 16.12
2.11–14, 3.4–7 We believe the grace of God – 14.23
3.4–7 Let us declare our faith in God's salvation – 14.24
3.5 God our Saviour shows *you* his kindness – 21.8

PHILEMON

1.3 Grace to you and peace from God – 3.21
1.3 Grace to you and peace from God – 16.13

HEBREWS

1.1–3 God who spoke to our ancestors – 14.25
1.2–3 This is Jesus – 19.12
1.3–8 Jesus is God's Son – 19.24
4.14–16 We have a great high priest – 4.5
4.12–13 Lord, before your eyes – 13.4
4.16 Let us approach God's throne – 15.2
5.2–10 Jesus is God's Son – 19.8
9.14 The blood of Christ – 21.9
9.28 Christ Jesus was sacrificed – 19.25
10.19–22 Since we have confidence – 5.22
10.22–23 Draw near with a sincere heart – 8.26
10.10 Christ Jesus was sacrificed – 19.25
10.23–25 Hold unswervingly to the hope you profess – 24.38
12.22–28 Come to Mount Zion – 4.6
12.22–28 Come to worship the Lord – 5.23
12.22–28 You have come to the heavenly Jerusalem – 2.19
12.1–2 Since *you* are surrounded by such a great cloud – 24.39
12.14 Make every effort to live in peace – 24.40
13.1–5 Keep on loving each other – 25.9
13.12–15 Jesus suffered outside the city gates – 25.10

JAMES

1.25 Do not merely listen to the word – 13.5
4.8–10 Come near to God – 4.7

1 PETER

1.2 Grace and peace be yours – 3.22
1.2 Grace and peace be yours – 16.14
1.25 The word of the Lord remains for ever – 12.12
1.25 This is the Gospel we proclaim – 12.13
1.3–14 Let us proclaim our faith – 14.26
3.18–22 Let us confess our faith in Christ – 14.27
2.9 We are a chosen people – 10.25
5.14–15 Greet one another with love's embrace – 3.23
5.14 Peace to all of you – 16.15
5.14 Greet one another with love's embrace – 16.16
5.7 Cast all your burdens on to Jesus – 21.10

Season and Subject Index

19.21 Jesus is the Living One (Revelation 1)
21.13 Look to Jesus and fall before him (Revelation 1)

CHRISTMAS – *see also 'Advent', 'Epiphany'*
2.3 Today in the town of David (Luke 2)
2.4 The Word became flesh (John 1)
19.11 Jesus is the Word of God (John 1)
19.12 This is Jesus (Hebrews 1)

CHURCH
2.18 We are the family of God (Ephesians 3)
3.5 Welcome one another (Romans 15)
3.6 To the church of God (1 Corinthians 1)
3.9 Peace and mercy to the people of God (Galatians 6)
5.6 Lord, thank you for this building (Psalm 26)
10.23 Sisters and brothers (Philippians 4)
10.25 We are a chosen people (1 Peter 2)
14.14 We are the family of God (Ephesians 3)
14.15 As God's people, let us declare our faith (Ephesians 4)
15.2 Let us approach God's throne (Hebrews 4, Ephesians 3)
16.4 To the church of God (1 Corinthians 1)
23.2 We declare this day (Deuteronomy 26)

COMMANDMENTS – *see chapter 6*
7.3 O Lord our God (Nehemiah 9)
7.12 Hear the words of Jesus (Psalm 119 and Mark 12)
7.27 Lord God almighty (Amos 2)
11.19 We see God's glory in the heavens (Psalm 19)
11.119(33) O Lord, teach me your commandments (Psalm 119)
11.119(145) O Lord, my heart cries out to you (Psalm 119)
11.119(169) O Lord, hear the cry of my heart (Psalm 119)
12.2 These are the Lord's words and laws (Exodus 24)
13.5 Do not merely listen to the word (James 1)
23.2 We declare this day (Deuteronomy 26)
23.4 Lord, you are my destiny (Psalm 119 (57)
23.5 Our Lord God, you are the only Lord (Mark 12)

COMMISSIONING – *see also 'ministry'*
24.3 *(Let us)* Rescue the poor who cry for help (Job 29)

COMMUNION – *see chapter 18*
1.5 The earth is the Lord's (Psalm 24)
4.8 Come, all who are thirsty (Isaiah 55)
5.4 Lord, we have faith in you (Psalm 78)
5.5 Lord God, we are here to worship you (Psalm 26)
5.6 Lord, thank you for this building (Psalm 26)
5.7 Lord, you are our light and our salvation (Psalm 27)
5.8 O God, you are our God (Psalm 63)
5.22 Since we have confidence (Hebrews 10)
19.25 Christ Jesus was sacrificed (Hebrews 9 and 10)
25.5 The *Communion/Supper/Eucharist/Mass* is ended (Luke 24)

CONFESSION – *see chapter 7*

6.7 Hear the commandments of the Lord (Exodus 20/Deuteronomy 5 and Psalm 106)

COVENANT
4.6 Come to Mount Zion (Hebrews 12)
5.22 Since we have confidence (Hebrews 10)
5.23 Come to worship the Lord (Hebrews 12)
7.23 O Lord, we acknowledge (Jeremiah 14)
12.1 This is the book of the Covenant (Exodus 24)

CREATION
1.5 The earth is the Lord's (Psalm 24)
4.1 Come, let's joyfully praise our God (Psalm 95)
5.2 We stand up and praise you (Nehemiah 9)
11.8 O Lord, our Lord (Psalm 8)
11.19 We see God's glory in the heavens (Psalm 19)
11.148 Praise the Lord (Psalm 148)

DEDICATION – see chapter 23
5.6 Lord, thank you for this building (Psalm 26)

EASTER
2.14 Christ has indeed been raised (1 Corinthians 15)
2.15 Jesus Christ is risen (1 Corinthians 15)
2.16 Christ is risen from the dead (Romans 8)
3.11 Wake up, sleepers (Ephesians 5)
14.9 We proclaim the Gospel (Romans 1)
14.30 We believe in Jesus Christ (Revelation 1)
14.31 Let us declare our faith in God (Revelation 1)
16.20 Grace and peace to you (Revelation 1)
19.5 This is Jesus (Luke 24)
19.18 This is Jesus (Luke 24)
19.19 Jesus is the Living One (Revelation 1)
19.20 Jesus is the faithful witness (Revelation 1)
19.21 Jesus is the Living One (Revelation 1)
24.34 Since *you* have been raised with Christ (Colossians 3)

EASTER SUNDAY
1.5 The earth is the Lord's (Psalm 24)

EPIPHANY
2.6 Arise, shine, for your light has come (Isaiah 60)
2.7 Jesus is born king of the Jews (Matthew 2)
2.8 Christ the light of the world (Luke 2)
14.9 We proclaim the Gospel (Romans 1)
19.13 Jesus is born king of the Jews (Matthew 2)
19.14 This is God's son (Matthew 4)
19.15 We have found the Christ (John 1)
19.16 Jesus is the Lamb of God (John 1)

ETERNAL LIFE
11.21 Lord, we rejoice in your strength (Psalm 21)
11.23 The Lord is my shepherd (Psalm 23)
13.3 To whom shall we go but Jesus (John 6)